The Pressed Flower
Picture Book

The Pressed Flower

The Art of Collecting, Pressing,
Arranging, and Framing
Garden and Wild Flowers
for Your Home

Picture Book

BY IRENE FLESHER
Illustrated by Glory Brightfield

Butterick Publishing

All poetry quotations are from *An Introduction to Haiku*, by Harold G. Henderson (Doubleday, 1958).

Technical drawings, chapter 9: Frank Flesher
Book design: Angela Foote
Photography: Edward Scibetta
Editor: Willa Speiser

Library of Congress Catalog Card Number: 77-92605
International Standard Book Number: 0-88421-056-1

For Rick and Glory and Savitri

Acknowledgements

Flowers and friends—what would we do without them? I am very grateful for having been blessed with both.

I probably would never have written this book without my beloved children, Rick and Glory Brightfield. When they saw the pictures I was making and the fun I had making them, they kept saying, "Write a book about it"—so I did.

And my husband Frank—you will read his chapter on frames. When I began dragging all those beat-up frames home from the flea markets and other places, he immediately set to work to find out how to salvage and repair them for me. Some of them really seemed hopeless but he always managed to fix them, and after he was through you would never have recognized them.

And Eleanor Brown, my friend and next-door neighbor for twenty years in Maryland. I'll never forget the first time I took my flower pictures over to Eleanor's house to show them to her. It's a strange feeling to show your creations for the first time. You get sort of a sinking feeling. You like what you have done, but will others like it?

Eleanor did not keep me in suspense. She really loved my pictures and began making plans for me to exhibit them. She helped me in every way she could. We went to flea markets together, church bazaars and second-hand shop looking for frames and velvet—she got her friends to give me the old frames they had in their attics. And she had a gift for creative criticism which was invaluable. She now lives far away in Las Vegas.

Then there is my life-time friend Mildred Knipp. She lives in Sarasota, Florida now, but she still sends her encouragement over the miles as she has always done in all my ventures.

Golena Brown, my helper and co-worker when I was in the restaurant business. She too has given me praise and encouragement, and although she is in Maryland and I am in New York, I can feel the strength of her good wishes.

Ruth Grover Burnstein way down there in Miami for all those letters wishing me well.

My brother Bill Pool, his wife Helen Pool, and their daughter Cathy Pool. They too are in Maryland, but they keep searching out frames for me, and help me in every way they can.

I miss them all.

And I want to thank all of the ladies of the Essex (Maryland) Library, and especially Evelyn Gresham, who was always on the lookout for books for me to read about flowers. All of the ladies of the library helped me by being enthusiastic about what I was doing, and their praise always made me work harder to try and deserve it.

So many friends have helped me in this way—Glory's mother, Ethel Lesser, who has a picture of mine hanging in her kitchen in Ohio, and says she thinks of me whenever she looks at it. And the young people of Woodstock—Iris and Phil Bresler and Kathy and Vinny Hars, Patty and Dick Friel of Hyde Park, Marion and Bill Ostrander, who were my next-door neighbors for all too short a time when I first moved here, and many, many more.

And I want to thank Willa Speiser and Ed Scibetta, my new young friends from Butterick. They worked long hours photographing my pictures, and I enjoyed every minute of working with them.

And last but not least my thanks to my father-in-law, Dr. Joseph Flesher, and my brother-in-law, Dr. Eugene Flesher, for the instruments they contributed to my hobby and which have been of such great help. And to Frank's brother, Joe Flesher, for his research into frame materials and sources of supplies.

The combination of flowers, help, love, and encouragement is a powerful one. With all of these anyone can accomplish anything.

Contents

Introducing Myself

My name is Irene Flesher, and I have lived on this earth for seventy years. I began making dried flower paintings five years ago and I have been making them ever since. I mention this fact because it may be interesting to know that a new hobby can be started at any age.

While browsing through the library shelves one day I came across a book on the art of making dried flower pictures. Any book about flowers attracts me, so I took it home, never dreaming that it would in many ways change my life. By change I mean that it made me see the world about me with new eyes, opening new doors and certainly making life more variable and exciting.

I sat down and read the book from cover to cover, and from that day on I was determined to learn how to create

11

my own flower pictures. Only books and experience taught me, and I think observation should also be added to these, because if you train yourself to see how flowers grow in the garden, how great artists have portrayed flowers, how flower arrangers have created lovely, though sadly, temporary pictures with fresh flowers, then you will have flower pictures in your mind when you sit down to work. I have explained this more fully in the chapter "Sources of Inspiration."

From the beginning, I read everything I could find on the subject and I still do. My first picture was done in fear and trembling. Can I do it? Will it work? At first I kept putting it off, saying, "I'll press a few more flowers before I begin," or "Today is not the day." You know how it is. Finally I just went to work and tried all the things I had read about. It wasn't long before I was experimenting and trying new ideas and having lots of fun in the process.

If, instead of learning this craft, which was completely new to me, I had decided it was too much trouble, think of all the fun I would have missed, and all the joy of creating something beautiful with the flowers I love so much.

People have said to me that they too would like to be able to make flower pictures, and then they give me reasons why they are not successful. They say, "My flowers press crooked," "I'm not artistic," "I don't have the time," or "My flowers lose their color." But if they sincerely wanted to create flower paintings, they could. I have lived long enough to know by now that you can do anything if you really want to.

In creating pressed flower pictures, the old saying "Experience is the best teacher" is true. It takes patience and perseverance, and there is more to it than meets the eye. Some paintings take shape right away, and others never do—it is the same as in any endeavor. Try and try again, and you will know when you have achieved the effect you want. Suddenly everything will fall into place, and you will have created a flower painting. It is an exhilarating feeling, worth striving and waiting for.

I have never done two pictures that are exactly alike. I do not think I could if I wanted to. Every flower and stem has its own individual way of growing, and it is best to let them dictate to you what form the picture will take. Really, sometimes they seem to be telling you what to do. When this happens, listen.

I have composed dried flower paintings that are like fantasy landscapes, others like flower borders in an English garden. Some are like old-fashioned bouquets, others like modern flower arrangements. I never know how they are going to turn out when I begin. I page through my assortment of flowers, grasses, and leaves, picking one here and one there, and suddenly a flower painting comes to life.

In this book, we've used the terms *flower painting* and *flower picture* interchangeably. One of the nicest compliments I can receive for my flower pictures is for someone to say, "They look just like paintings." When someone says this I feel that I have achieved that certain something I am always striving for. To me it means that it is more than a good picture—it is a painting created with flowers that will live forever.

So if you think you too would like to create dried flower paintings, there is only one way to find out whether you will find it a fascinating hobby or not—try it. I will share what I have learned and all my secrets with you.

I. F.
Chichester, New York
August, 1977

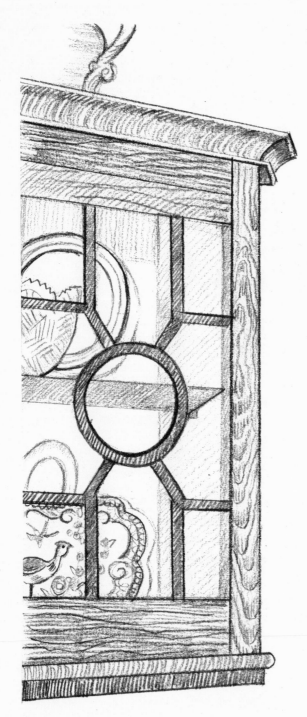

A pressed flower picture hanging next to an antique what-not hand made by an old sea captain.

First Things First

The first thing to do when you decide you are going to create dried flower paintings is to collect the flowers. Flowers, grasses, weeds, and leaves are all around you. All you need to press them is a pressing book—any book with absorbent paper will do (I use copies of *Organic Gardening,* a magazine published by Rodale Press)—a small pair of scissors, and the gift, which can be developed, of seeing nature's beauty all around you. The material for the picture can be gathered in a very short time, even in a park in the middle of a busy city. I do not mean that you should pick the flowers growing there, which are for everyone's enjoyment, but weeds and grasses are abundant everywhere, and probably no one would object to your picking them.

The ideal way to obtain your flowers is to have a little garden of your own. Even a small flower border will give

15

you a wealth of flowers to work with. One plant of Johnny-jump-ups, one of coralbells, and some wild daisies and a few grasses will supply enough material to create a picture.

I saw some lovely dried flower pictures on display once in a library in Maryland. They were made by a lady who obtained all her material from a friend's garden. They were almost entirely made of pansies because this flower was her friend's specialty.

The fields and waysides are full of material. Queen Anne's lace grows everywhere. If you do have a garden, try growing some from seed. The cultivated kind is even lovelier than the wild kind—bigger and whiter, and easy to grow and press. Goldenrod and buttercups grow everywhere, too, as do many other prolific wild flowers. Graceful grasses, dainty weeds, and ferns are easy to find. They are as beautiful as cultivated flowers and are free for the taking.

Some plants are protected by conservation lists and must not be picked. Native dogwood and mountain laurel, for example, may not be picked in New York State when found growing wild. Native cypripedium, or wild orchids, must also be left growing. I have never seen these orchids on my walks in the woods. You can often find plants that are on the prohibited list at wild flower nurseries, however. There you can order all sorts of beautiful wild flowers and plant them on your own property, then pick and press them. In Maryland I grew the foam flower and loved its dainty little sprays. I do not have it in New York, but I intend to plant it next year. This is one of the nice things about flower pictures—you're always planning for the future.

Remember, too, when you do pick wild flowers and plants, that you should pick them carefully—don't pull them up by the roots.

I am always searching for a new flower, a new weed, new leaves. I love the various shapes of leaves and their many shades of green. Collecting leaves could be a hobby in itself. This search is a fascinating pastime, and it can make you realize that you have never before really observed the world around you, especially when you get down on your hands and knees and look at the abundance of green things growing in profusion in the fields and woods. It is important to carry a pressing book with you always. Weeds—I do not like to call them by this name, because they are often so beautiful—fade very quickly if not pressed immediately.

The short life of picked wild flowers is the best reason for growing your own flowers, I think. You can choose the ideal time to pick them. This is the middle of a bright, sunny, dry day. You should pick them at their peak, just as they are coming into full bloom. Buds are an exception to this. Pick as many as you can find of these, because they really do something special for a picture.

I carry a small basket with me when picking flowers in my own garden, and I pick only enough at one time so that I can press them all creatively and immediately. I arrange them on pressing paper, then put them in a dark place with a weight on top, and leave them undisturbed for a week or more. They are then ready and waiting to help me create lovely flower paintings. Flowers pressed this way will stay colorful even after a number of years.

If you do decide to grow your own flowers, what kind will you grow? There is such a wealth to choose from, it is not easy to decide.

Everyone has his or her favorite flower. Mine is larkspur. To me it is the queen of flowers for pressing. It has such a dainty shape, and it comes in such gorgeous colors—all shades of pink, lavender, purple, and white. It holds its color well and combines with other flowers in such a graceful way. And I love all daisies. The daisy form seems to be especially suited to dried flower pictures. They very often give a lovely lift to a picture. If you are having trouble

Hanging baskets above my kitchen sink—a gesneriad, a grape ivy, and a begonia.

with an arrangement, try adding a daisy here and there and see what happens.

I love all flowers, of course, but not all of them press well. You have to keep experimenting. I love to try new flowers. It is exciting to see how they turn out, and there is always the chance that you will discover something outstanding and different. This is the way I discovered two flowers that never appear on any of the lists of flowers considered good for pressing. They are tomato blossoms and strawberry blossoms. Tomato blossoms have a deep yellow color and an attractive star shape. Strawberry blossoms have a creamy color and an appealing round shape. I use both of these blossoms often because they press well, hold their color, and always look interesting.

Every year I try to add a few new flowers to my repertoire. I discovered celosia this way—by trying it. It is a wonderful flower for pressing, holds its color, and develops unusual shapes. Both the feathery celosia and the fan-shaped celosia are lovely and arrange well.

At the end of this chapter you will find a list of all the flowers I have ever pressed. The list tells you whether they are annual or perennial, their color, consistency, and texture—thin, medium, or thick—and what I have found out about each one, as far as pressing is concerned. It includes grasses, wild flowers, houseplants, herbs, shrubs, and bulbs. There are still many flowers I have not pressed, but I hope to try them all some day. I always start my list for next year as soon as the snow starts falling.

If you can't have a garden of your own, please don't give up. There are so many ways to obtain flowers. If you have a sunny window you could grow a few flowering plants just for picking. Another source—if you are rich—is a florist shop. The one and only kind of flower I buy from a florist is mimosa. The mimosa we get probably comes from the South, where it blooms early. Mimosa has many small yellow buttons and comes in graceful sprays. A small bunch goes a long way. You can usually find mimosa in the florist shops in February.

Whether you grow your own flowers, or pick them from a friend's garden, the fields and woods, windowsill, or florist, you will soon have all the material you need to work with if you have a regular routine of picking a few blossoms every sunny day and storing them away. You will be surprised how quickly you can accumulate plenty of material for creating lovely flower paintings.

IN SEARCH OF WILD FLOWERS

I have just brought home a book from the library called *Wild Flowers of America*. It has 400 beautiful paintings of wild flowers from every part of America—from the warm to the cold regions. It is published by the Smithsonian Institution in Washington, D.C., and it is the very best book on wild flowers I have found so far. The paintings are lovely and so clear that you can easily recognize a flower you are familiar with but whose name you do not know. The book enabled me to finally identify the wild flower jewelweed. I saw it for the first time here in New York, but no one could tell me its name.

Also in *Wild Flowers of America,* I learned that tillandsia grows wild in southern Florida. I grow this indoors as an exotic houseplant and look forward to the day when it will bloom. It has lovely blue flowers, covered with red- and purple-tinged scales—and it presses beautifully. A field of it must be a sensational sight.

Many of the flowers listed I have taken for granted all my life—goldenrod, chicory, buttercup, oxeye daisy—to name only a few. I remember some exquisite wild flowers that grew in the woods in back of our home in Maryland when I was a child. Anemones and spring beauty used to grow at the foot of certain trees. I knew where they were and used to go looking for them every spring. Waxy white bloodroots bloomed in the spring beside a stream, and there was a special place where I went to pick violets like I've never seen since. They were pale lavender and a deep velvety purple combined. Once when I was grown up I tried to find them again, but they were gone. If only I had pressed some long ago and saved them for today.

Here in New York I have become acquainted with new wild flowers that delight me—butter-and-eggs, jewelweed, bee balm, viper's bugloss, hypericum, elderberry, mouse-ear, the shadblow tree, and many others growing profusely by the wayside. The wild flowers here are the loveliest I have ever seen.

I am looking at the flowers in this book and dreaming. Wouldn't it be wonderful to get in the car and start driving westward across the United States, picking and pressing wild flowers as one traveled? Since this is impossible, I will have to order and grow some of the unusual flowers in my own backyard.

Flowers I Have Pressed

This is my list of all the flowers and leaves I have pressed, and what I think of each one. I am going to tell you whether they press in a thin, medium, or thick way; whether they can be color washed; and if they are annual, perennial, shrub, wild flower, herb, or bulb.

If you have never pressed flowers before you will not know what the texture and quality will be until the pressing is completed. It is sometimes a help to know beforehand. After you have pressed a number of flowers you will usually recognize at a glance how they will turn out.

I find this knowledge useful because I have found that you can achieve different effects with flower textures. Thin flowers on silk, paper, or emory cloth look as if they have been painted on with watercolors; medium flowers combine with both thin and thick flowers to obtain interesting effects; and thick flowers on velvet often look as if they have been embroidered or sculptured.

I have not put down the length of time it takes to press each flower. This depends on where you live, and whether the weather is dry or damp. I have found that it is best to wait at least a week before opening your pressing papers. Most flowers are finished in this length of time, but if they are still not completely dry (unless you want to color wash them at this time), put them gently back and wait another two or three days. It depends a lot on the texture of the flowers. Thin flowers will often be completely dry in a couple of days. Medium flowers usually take a week. Thick flowers may even take two weeks to dry.

FLOWER LIST

ABUTILON

ABUTILON
(Flowering Maple)

Houseplant, medium. Does not always turn out well, but when it does it is interesting. Cut out hard center before pressing. Color wash carefully.

ACHIMENES

Bulb, thin. Best pressed sideways. Color wash with care.

ACHIMENES

ACHILLIA

ACHILLIA

Perennial. There are several kinds. "The Pearl," with thick, small white flowers, is the one I have grown.

AFRICAN VIOLET

AFRICAN VIOLET

Houseplant, presses paper thin, but stamens stay yellow and are very prominent. Does not hold its color and does not color wash well. This was disappointing for me because I love African violets and they come in lovely colors. I still always press a few in hopes I can use them someplace.

ALLIUM
(Flowering Onion)

ALLIUM

Perennial bulb. Presses beautifully and comes out looking like silk. It is too thin to be color-washed. I have only pressed the white, but it also comes in blue, yellow, and rose.

ALYSSUM

A joy and a delight, not only for pressing, but in the garden. They thrive without having to be pampered and the annual kind are deliciously perfumed. Two kinds:

1. Sweet Alyssum: annual, thin. White, pink, lavender, rose. Press in small sprays. Color wash.
2. Alyssum (Basket-of-Gold): perennial, thin. A pretty yellow. Press each little stem with flowers. Color-wash.

ALYSSUM

ANCHUSA

ANCHUSA

Perennial forget-me-not (there is also an annual kind), medium. Presses well and can be color washed.

ANEMONE

ANEMONE
(Blanda)

Bulb. This is a dainty daisy-like flower. It is quite different from the showy anemone most people are acquainted with, which does not press well. Blanda presses thin but not too thin. Leaves are pretty, too. Color wash.

APPLE BLOSSOM

APPLE BLOSSOM

Tree, medium. If pressed when blossoms first open they are very lovely—white with shades of purple and yellow stamens. Small sprays of leaves can be pressed, too. Color wash.

AQUILIGIA

AQUILIGIA
(Columbine)

Thin, presses well. All colors and interesting shapes, press leaves, too. Press some flowers sideways. Color wash.

ARCTOTIS
(African Daisy)

Annual, petals press very thin, center thick—do not always turn out, but are worth a try. Petals cannot be color washed.

ASPARAGUS

Perennial vegetable, medium. Graceful little sprays, good filler-in. Color wash.

ASTER

Perennial. The small ones press the best (center is hard and must be pressed down when placed for pressing). Looks like a colored daisy and comes in lavender, purple, white, blue. The little purple wild kind presses well if picked when it first comes into bloom, and the centers are yellow. Color wash.

ASTILBE
(Spirea)

Perennial, thick. Presses well, white, pink, blue. A very good spear form, useful for establishing a line. Color wash.

AZALEA

Shrub, thin. Loses color and is hard to color wash—in other words, temperamental, but try some anyway.

BABY'S BREATH

Annual and perennial, medium, dainty white or pink sprays. This, too, is useful as a filler, just as it is used in fresh-flower arrangements. Color wash. I prefer the perennials.

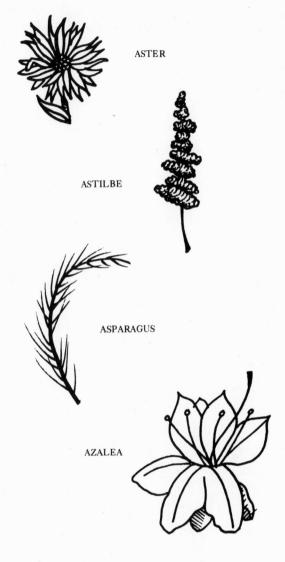

ASTER

ASTILBE

ASPARAGUS

AZALEA

BABY'S BREATH

BABY'S TEARS

BACHELOR'S BUTTON

BAPTISIA

BEE BALM

BEGONIA

BABY'S TEARS

Houseplant. Dainty, leafy little plant. Very pretty used as a focal point in a small picture to represent the forest floor. Thin. Color wash.

BACHELOR'S BUTTON
(Cornflower)

Annual, medium, blue, pink, violet, white, rose. Raggedy edges give an unusual outline. Color wash. Be sure to pick when they first come into bloom or they will shatter.

BAPTISIA

Perennial, medium. Interesting blue spikes; not too easy to work into an arrangement, but try it because there are times when it is just the thing you are looking for. Color wash.

BEE BALM
(Bergamot)

Perennial or wild flower, medium to thick. I have only pressed the wild, purple kind so far; it is lovely. Press sideways for a bold, striking effect. Color wash.

BEGONIA

Houseplant. Presses well but is very thin and papery, and turns brown. Cannot be color washed. However, if you decide to work out a painting with browns on a light background it can be very effective. Leaves can be pressed, too, but they also press very thin.

BLACK-EYED SUSAN VINE

Annual or houseplant, orange and yellow. Makes a lovely hanging basket. Presses very thin, but has a trumpet shape with an interesting touch of black. Color does not hold well and it is hard to color wash. It turns a creamy sort of color; the leaves and stems are graceful and unusual, too.

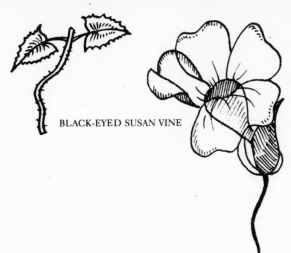

BLACK-EYED SUSAN VINE

BLADDER CAMPION

Wild flower. Interesting and graceful. Green and lavender shaded. Color wash.

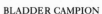

BLEEDING HEART
(Pink)

Perennial, medium. This is very pretty and I like it, but for some reason it died out in my garden. I'll try it again. Color wash.

BLADDER CAMPION

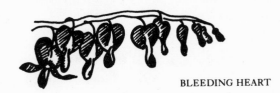

BLEEDING HEART

BLUE LACE FLOWER

Annual, medium. Looks like Queen Anne's but it is blue. Look closely—it really looks like lace. Color wash.

BLUE LACE FLOWER

BOUGAINVILLEA

BORAGE

BRACHYCOME

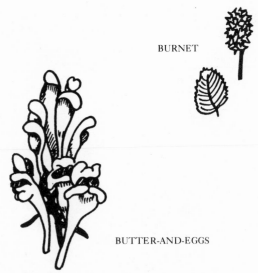

BRIDAL WREATH

BURNET

BUTTER-AND-EGGS

BOUGAINVILLEA

Houseplant in the North, grows profusely in the South, presses medium. White, pink, and red are the only colors I have used. Color wash.

BORAGE

Annual herb, but reseeds every year; presses too thin and shiny. This was a disappointment to me because the flower is such a lovely blue and has a true star shape. I always press some and use them wherever I can. Do not color wash.

BRACHYCOME
(Swan River daisy)

Annual, thin. A pretty little daisy in blue, rose, white. Foliage presses well, too. Color wash.

BRIDAL WREATH

Shrub, thick. Press in sprays and gently color wash. Sometimes looks like little trees.

BURNET

Perennial herb. Interesting leaves, a small, strange flower. Pick and press it just as it is coming into bloom. Do not color wash.

BUTTER-AND-EGGS

Wild flower, medium, yellow with a touch of orange. Small but effective with a silky texture. Press individually or in sprays, press foliage, too. If flowers sometimes turn out to be jet black do not be surprised—as I was—it does not happen often. Color wash.

BUTTERCUP

Wild flower, medium, one of my favorites. Holds its silky, yellow color well. I only press the single kind but it comes in double, too. I sometimes color wash the back of the petals, but it is not really necessary. Do not color wash front of flower, you will ruin its luster.

BUTTERCUP

BUTTERFLY WEED

Perennial, thick. Has beautiful yellow and orange flowers that press like little fans; very useful for focal points. Color wash.

BUTTERFLY WEED

CALLIOPSIS

Annual, thin, daisy shape and bright colors—yellow, yellow and brown, red, orange. Presses well. Color wash.

CALLIOPSIS

CAMOMILE

Perennial herb, medium, little white daisies and pretty foliage. Color wash.

 CAMOMILE

CANDYTUFT

Annual or perennial, another great flower for pressing. The perennial kind is white. The annual kind comes in many colors—red, lavender, blue, violet, and white. Color wash.

CANDYTUFT

CELOSIA

CELOSIA

Annual, medium to thick, unusual shapes. Holds color well, but can be color washed if you want to be sure.

Two kinds:

1. Plume type: feathery spikes in gold, red, orange, and one in silvery white.
2. Crested type: dwarf ones are the best for pressing, red, yellow, orange. Makes an excellent focal point. Press leaves, too, but be sure both flowers and leaves are completely free of moisture since this flower does not press well if it is the least bit damp.

CELANDINE

CELANDINE

Annual, grows wild in England, but I grow it from seed. It is a lovely little yellow and white flower with a pretty center. Can be color washed with care, but perhaps it is best to leave it alone, because it turns a pretty cream color when it fades.

CHERRY BLOSSOMS

CHERRY BLOSSOMS

Tree. Must be picked when just coming into bloom or it will turn brown. Color wash.

CHRYSANTHEMUM

Perennial, thick. I press both single and double. Yellow, white, and pink are the only colors I have pressed. The double small ones give a water-lily effect at times and make a perfect focal flower. Color wash.

CHRYSANTHEMUM

CLARKIA

CLARKIA

Annual, thin. It has been my experience that it does not always press well, but when it does, I love it. Color wash with care, if at all.

CLEMATIS

Perennial vine, medium. Interesting flowers that turn brown; leaves and tendrils should be pressed, too.

CLEMATIS

CLEOME

CLEOME

Annual, presses tissue thin but looks wonderful against dark velvet. Pink or white. Cannot be color washed.

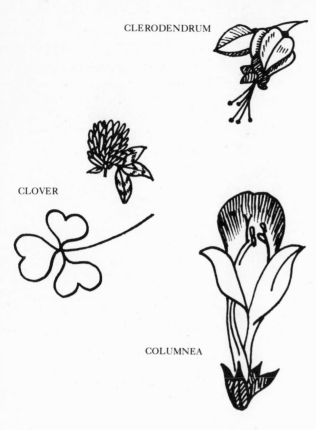

CLOVER

COLUMNEA

CLERODENDRUM
(Glory-bower)

Houseplant, medium. Unusual white flowers, press seperately. Color wash.

CLOVER

Wild flower, white and red, leaves press thin, flowers thick. Both leaves and flowers press well. Color wash.

COLUMNEA

Houseplant, medium. Trumpet-like yellow flower. Color wash.

COSMOS

Annual, medium. Presses beautifully, yellow, rose, white. Holds color well, but can be color washed.

COREOPSIS

Perennial, medium, gold, pretty. One plant will supply you with all the flowers you can use. Color wash.

COREOPSIS

CORIANDER

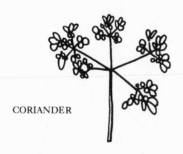

CORIANDER

Annual herb, thin, pretty lavender circles. Color wash.

CORALBELLS

Perennial, medium. Pink or white sprays. A very useful flower to have on hand. Presses well. Color wash.

CORALBELLS

CREPE MYRTLE

Shrub in the South, houseplant in the North, thin, pink but dries lavender. Color wash.

CROCUS

Bulb, silky and thin. Cannot be color washed.

CROCUS

CROWN OF THORNS

Houseplant, medium. Tiny bright red flowers hold color well and are easy to color wash.

CROWN OF THORNS

CUCUMBER FLOWERS

Annual vegetable. A thin, yellow, nicely shaped flower that can be color washed.

CUCUMBER FLOWERS

DAISY

DAISY

The kind that grows profusely everywhere (sometimes called field daisy, or oxeye daisy). The smaller ones seem to press best for me—petals thin, center thick. Color wash.

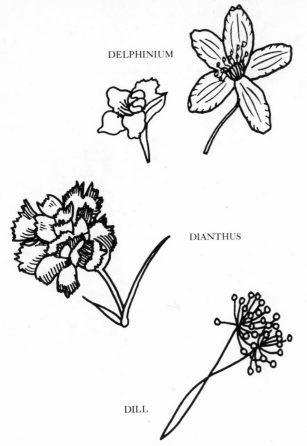

DELPHINIUM

DIANTHUS

DILL

DELPHINIUM

Medium, perennial. If you can get them to grow they are wonderful, especially the blue ones, very much like larkspur but perennial and larger. Very temperamental in the garden for me. Color wash.

DIANTHUS
(Pink)

Medium, all colors. I like the ones that look like lace. Color wash with care.

DILL

Annual herb, medium, pretty yellow circles. Color wash.

DORONICUM

Perennial, medium. A beautiful yellow daisy that holds color well if picked just as it comes into bloom. Also, color washes very well.

ELDERBERRY FLOWERS

ELDERBERRY FLOWERS

Shrub, medium, beautiful creamy sprays. Can be color washed, but not necessary.

EMILIA
(Paintbrush)

Annual, thick. Interesting flower—retains curves and is graceful. Press with stems. Easy to color wash.

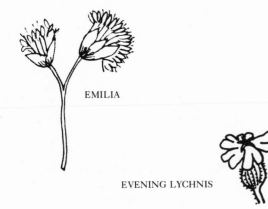

EMILIA

EVENING LYCHNIS

EVENING LYCHNIS

Wild flower. I found this in New York growing wild in my garden. Press sideways. Color wash carefully or not at all.

EVENING PRIMROSE

EVENING PRIMROSE

Perennial, thin, shiny. Silky yellow flowers. Presses well but cannot be color washed.

FATSIA JAPONICA

FATSIA JAPONICA

Houseplant, medium. Press small leaves only. They will turn jet black, no need to color wash.

FERNS

Wild or houseplants, thin to medium. I grow my own. My favorites are the maidenhair fern and the button fern. Color wash.

FERNS

FORSYTHIA

Shrub, thin. A nice yellow but turns cream and cannot be color washed. Presses in little bell shapes.

FORSYTHIA

FUCHSIA

FUCHSIA

Houseplant in winter, in the garden in summer, lovely colors. Presses very well (press sideways). Color wash.

GERANIUM

GERANIUM

Houseplant in winter, grows outside in summer. I like the buds and leaves better than the flowers, which do not hold their color and are hard to color wash.

GOLDENGLOW

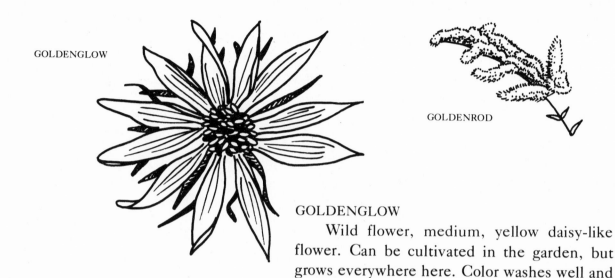

GOLDENROD

GRAPE LEAF IVY

GRAPE LEAVES

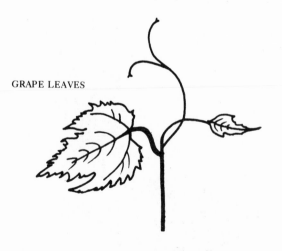

GOLDENGLOW

Wild flower, medium, yellow daisy-like flower. Can be cultivated in the garden, but grows everywhere here. Color washes well and makes an ideal focus-point flower.

GOLDENROD

Wild flower, medium to thick. One of the very best wild flowers to press and so plentiful it is no problem to find. Press in sprays. Color wash.

GRAPE LEAF IVY

Houseplant, thin. This is very much like the wild grape vine. Grows well in the house and is always on hand to pick and press if you need it.

GRAPE LEAVES

Cultivated or wild vine, thin. The small leaves with stems and tendrils make interesting lines. I try to find the ones growing at the very tip of the vine.

GRASSES

All kinds—you can find them anywhere. I grow two kinds in the garden.

1. Lagurus ovatus (Hare's Tail Grass) presses well and is always admired and exclaimed over.
2. Feather Grass (Stipa pennata) is a very delicate graceful grass.

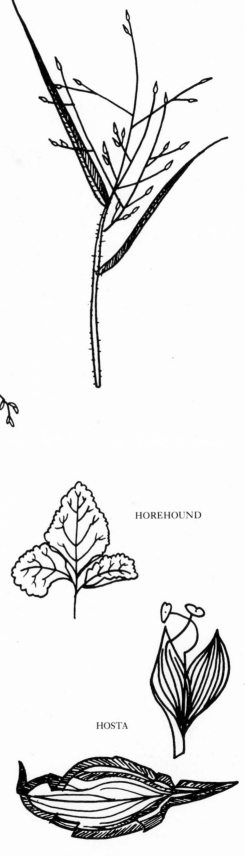

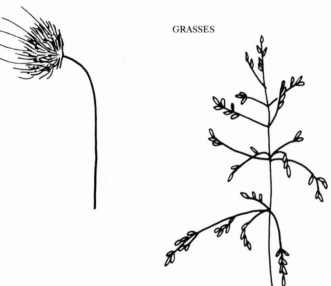

GRASSES

HOREHOUND

Perennial herb. Silvery leaves that press well. Texture is velvety. No need to color wash.

HOREHOUND

HOSTA
(Plantain lily)

Perennial, medium. Press flowers sideways. Press small leaves, which are more interesting than the flowers. They assume unusual shapes and sometimes stay green and white, or at times turn a lovely yellow.

HOSTA

HOYA

HYDRANGEA

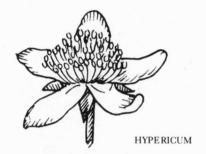

HYPERICUM

JEWELWEED

HOYA

Houseplant, thick little brown stars with another shiny little star in the center that looks like a jewel. Do not color wash.

HYDRANGEA

Shrub, medium. Press individual flowers. Color wash.

HYPERICUM
(St.-John's-Wort)

Wild flower or cultivated perennial. A beautiful, silky yellow with gorgeous stamens that look stunning against a dark velvet background. Cannot be color washed.

JEWELWEED

Wild flower. A delicate orange trumpet. It looks like it could not be color washed but it can be.

JOHNNY-JUMP-UPS

JOHNNY-JUMP-UPS
(Viola)

Perennial, thin. Adorable little flowers with faces like pansies, but they are smaller and easier to arrange than pansies. Color wash. Press some leaves, too. They turn a brilliant green.

KALANCHOE

Houseplant, medium. A brilliant orange flower that presses well and can be color washed.

LARKSPUR

KALANCHOE

LARKSPUR

Annual, medium. My favorite. Lovely colors, lovely forms, lovely buds and sprays, always graceful and obliging. I always think of this flower as being "on stage"—a real actress, loves "makeup." Press in sprays and singly.

LAVENDER

Perennial herb, thick lavender flowers. Color wash.

LAVENDER

LAZY DAISY

Annual, medium, A pretty little daisy.

LAZY DAISY

LEONTOPDIUM

An Alpine wild flower, satiny white, lovely. If you can't go climbing mountains for it, you may be able to grow it in your garden if you are lucky. Presses rather thick. Does not need to be color washed.

LEONTOPDIUM

LILY OF THE VALLEY

LILY OF THE VALLEY

Perennial, medium. Turns a creamy white and then brown, but if you color wash it in time, it retains its creaminess. Press in sprays; the little bells are attractive.

LUPIN

Perennial, medium, pink and purple. Press individual florets, leaves too—they are more interesting than the flowers, I think. Color wash.

LUPIN

MAPLE LEAVES

MAPLE LEAVES

Tree or you can raise it as a houseplant and bonsai it—that is, keep it small. Do not allow it to grow big. Small maple leaves are always interesting and the red and yellow ones you find in the fall are colorful. Color wash.

MARIGOLD

Annual, thick. I only press the very small ones, yellow, red, orange. Color wash.

MARIGOLD

MEADOW-RUE

Wildflower. I found this growing in a vacant lot across from my home—it has feathery, creamy, delicate sprays. The leaves are pretty too. Color wash the leaves but not the flowers.

MEADOW-RUE

MIMOSA

MIMOSA

Shrub, medium. Little yellow buttons in graceful sprays. This is the one flower I buy from a florist in the spring. Can be color washed but I usually do not; the buttons eventually turn brown but they are still pretty.

MOCK ORANGE

MOCK ORANGE

Shrub, medium, white flowers with yellow stamens. Presses well. Color wash.

MULLEIN

MULLEIN

Wild herb. Flowers are yellow and press thin and cannot be color washed. The leaves are the best part of the plant to press—they are a soft, velvety gray and are unbelievably beautiful against dark velvet.

MY LADY'S MANTLE

MY LADY'S MANTLE

Perennial herb, medium, yellowish-brown sprays and pretty leaves. Not necessary to color wash.

NARCISSUS

Bulb, medium. Small ones press best. There are many different kinds. Color wash.

NARCISSUS

NASTURTIUM

Thin and silky. Flowers do not always press well but buds do. Leaves press well, too, but turn yellow. Only the buds can be color washed.

NASTURTIUM

OKRA LEAF

ORCHID

OXYPETALUM

OKRA LEAF

Annual vegetable, medium. Only the tiny, young leaves should be pressed; they have interesting markings. Color wash.

ORCHID

Houseplant, thin. The large ones definitely cannot be pressed, but small ones press well. I once grew one called the buttonhole orchid. It had a small orange flower that pressed well and held its color. I'm sorry to say I lost it in moving from Maryland to New York.

OXYPETALUM

Annual, medium. Does not keep its pretty blue color, but can be color washed. Interesting shapes—look like child's drawings.

PALM

Houseplant. Press only small leaves. Color wash.

PALM

PANSY

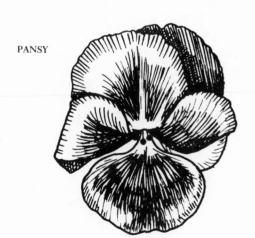

PANSY

Annual, thin. Presses very well and can be color washed. The large ones seem stiff to me and hard to arrange; I prefer violas.

PHLOX

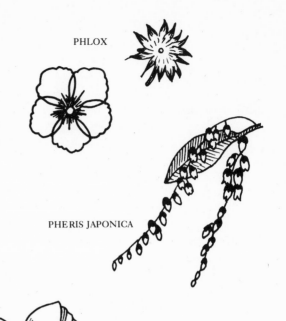

PHLOX

Annual and perennial. Very thin but can be color washed if done with care. The sprays of the perennial creeping phlox are pretty.

PIERIS JAPONICA
(Lily of the valley bush)

Shrub, medium, pretty creamy sprays. Color wash.

PHERIS JAPONICA

POPPY

Annual and perennial, paper thin. Very silky, hard to press but worth trying. Do not color wash.

POPPY

POTENTILLA

Annual and wild flower. A nice, round shape that presses well. Wild ones are yellow, the cultivated ones are a bright carmine-rose. Color wash.

POTENTILLA

QUEEN ANNE'S LACE

Wild flower or annual. Someone once said that if this flower were not so prolific it would cost a fortune. It is beautiful; really seems to like being pressed; arranges well; looks stunning against a dark background. Try growing the cultivated kind in your garden. It is easy to grow and is whiter and bigger than the wild kind, but also pick the wild kind—they are both exquisite. Color wash lightly with either white poster paint or Chinese white.

QUEEN ANNE'S LACE

RASPBERRY LEAF

RASPBERRY

Perennial fruit. Flower is not good for pressing, but the interesting-shaped leaves are. They are gray and do not need color washing.

ROSE

Shrub, thick if double, thin if single. Presses well but turns brown; pretty in a brown picture. I have only tried the white and yellow ones. Do not color wash.

ROSE

ROSEMARY

ROSEMARY

Herb, medium. Plant outside in summer but grow as a houseplant in the winter in cold climates. Flowers do not amount to much, but foliage is excellent—has interesting lines. Do not color wash.

SALVIA
(Sage)

Annual and perennial. I like all the salvias I have tried. There are many different kinds and

I want to try them all. These are the ones I have pressed:

SALVIA CLARY
Biennial, medium, lovely colors. Easy to color wash.

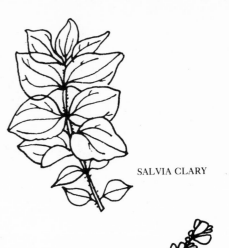

SALVIA CLARY

SALVIA FARINACEA
Perennial. A wonderful blue with touches of white—even the stems are blue. Color wash.

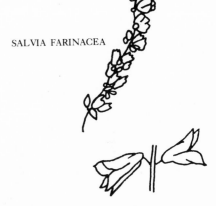

SALVIA FARINACEA

SALVIA SCARLET SAGE
Annual, medium, and the very best and brightest red color you can find. Color wash.

SALVIA SCARLET SAGE

SEAWEED

SEAWEED
A water plant. Gather this if you are lucky enough to find some. I found it growing in the river in front of my lawn in Maryland. Delicate and graceful. Do not color wash.

SHADBLOW

SHRIMP PLANT

SHADBLOW

Tree. The first tree to bloom here in the spring—you see it all over the mountains. Small, white starlike flower. Pick sprays of buds first and then some of the open flowers. Foliage is pretty too. Color wash.

SHRIMP PLANT

Houseplant, thick. Unusual colors—red, greens, orange—but too thick to arrange well. I have used it at times. Color wash.

SMILAX

SMILAX

Houseplant, thin. Trailing vine with satiny, small leaves which turn yellow after a time. Do not color wash.

SNAPDRAGON

Annual, medium. I like yellow the best. Presses well—press singly or in sprays. Color wash.

SNAPDRAGON

SNOWDROP GALANTHUS

Bulb. Pretty little white flower. Color wash.

SNOWDROP GALANTHUS

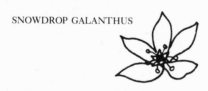

SNOWFLAKE LEUCOJUM

Bulb, medium. Also a pretty little white flower. Color wash.

SNOWFLAKE LEUCOJUM

SNOW-ON-THE-MOUNTAIN

SNOW-ON-THE-MOUNTAIN

Annual, medium. Green and white leaves. Flower is quite small and rather insignificant, but if you look closely you will see that it has a center that looks like a star. Color wash.

STAR-OF-BETHLEHEM

STAR-OF-BETHLEHEM

Bulb, thin. A star made of green silk. Do not color wash.

STRAWBERRY BLOSSOM

STRAWBERRY BLOSSOM

Perennial fruit, medium. Presses very well. Flowers are round, creamy white with a yellow center; leaves press well, too. Color wash.

SWEET PEA

SWEET PEA

Annual, thin. Color fades quickly. Texture like crepe de Chine. Cannot be color washed. Buds press better than open flowers.

TANSY

TANSY

Perennial herb, thick. Not unlike mimosa but yellow buttons are thicker and not as graceful. Color wash.

TARRAGON

Perennial herb, medium. Very graceful lines. Color wash.

TARRAGON

THYME

THYME

Perennial herb, medium. Little sprays with tiny lavender flowers can be pressed. Color wash.

TOMATO BLOSSOMS

TOMATO BLOSSOMS

Annual vegetable, medium. Presses very well. Interesting star shape and a lovely yellow color. Color wash.

VERBENA

Annual, thin, many colors. Pretty, but cannot be color washed.

TILLANDSIA

Houseplant. Very exotic flower—purple and red. Color wash.

VIPER'S BUGLOSS

Annual and wild flower, a nice blue color. I planted this in my garden this year and then found that it grows wild everywhere here. An unusual flower and foliage, and useful as a filler. Color wash.

VIOLET

Wild flower. A disappointment. Loses its color and does not press well. It is a small flower to start with and shrinks to nothing in the pressing.

VERBENA

TILLANDSIA

VIPER'S BUGLOSS

WOODRUFF

Perennial herb. Flowers are quite small but leaves are pretty. Color wash.

WOODRUFF

WEEDS

They grow everywhere and press well. Most can be color washed. Just keep looking for them wherever you go. I have found some beauties in front of the supermarket.

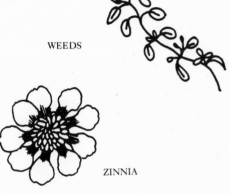

WEEDS

ZINNIA

Annual, thick, pretty colors. I use only the small ones. Color wash.

ZINNIA

Well, there they are. These are the flowers and leaves I have used in my flower pictures so far. Some of the weeds I have picked I have not listed individually because I do not know their names. To find graceful weeds, all you have to do is go for a walk or look around your own back yard. There are many more flowers that I want to press, and I will keep planting new ones and looking for weeds, grasses, and wild flowers wherever I may be.

My son Rick has a field next to his house, and it is alive with wild flowers. Whenever the weather is good, my daughter-in-law Glory and my four-year-old granddaughter Savitri and I take walks looking and searching. We carry a pressing book and a pair of scissors, and we pick and press as we go along. Savitri is becoming quite an expert at finding flowers, and she is really interested. It is fun, and a very healthful, together thing to do. I like to think that someday she will remember these flower-gathering walks and will perhaps create her own pressed flower paintings.

An oriental stand in front of which parade china figurines, from China.

Tools and Materials

Creating a dried flower picture is not unlike baking a cake. All the necessary tools and ingredients must be at hand before you begin. As in all creative projects, it helps to have the proper tools.

· You will need first of all a large working surface. It could be the kitchen or dining room table, or a desk, or a long board nailed to the wall. It should be big enough to hold your tools, your stack of dried flower papers, and the prepared frame you are using for your picture.

You will only need two tools for arranging flowers, leaves, and stems on the background of your picture. These two are for picking up and putting down your dried material.

· Tweezers or dental pliers, if you can find them.

· Any thin-pointed instrument—a thin bamboo stick (these are sold in most Oriental stores), a nail file, a metal meat skewer, or, best of all, one of those dental instruments of torture, one with a thin point on both ends.

Recently I fell heir to some old dental tools that are perfect for this sort of work. Luckily I have both a brother-in-law and a father-in-law who are dentists. If you are not lucky enough to have a dentist in the family the other tools will work just as well. You will probably find new tools that I have not thought of.

· I keep a roll of cellophane tape handy when I am arranging dried flowers because inevitably I will drop tiny bits of debris on the velvet and I like to clean up as I go along. This saves a lot of work when I have finished.

When I first began to make dried flower pictures I used a metal meat skewer and a nail file. I soon found, however, that I could control the placing of my material best with tweezers. If two flowers are close together and you want to move one but do not wish to disturb the other one tweezers will do the best job of moving without disturbing them. For gently pushing flowers into place a thin instrument is best.

I also keep a small pair of scissors handy while I am arranging and creating a flower picture. Sometimes a stem will be too long or too thick and must be clipped a little. More about this later.

To sum it up, I use the tweezers for lifting and placing the flowers on the velvet. When I think the picture is finished I gently push everything exactly in place with my pointed tool. This is all you need for the actual arranging of your picture.

You will need another set of tools for color washing, which will follow after you have decided that your picture is complete and ready for the magic touch that keeps it fresh and lovely.

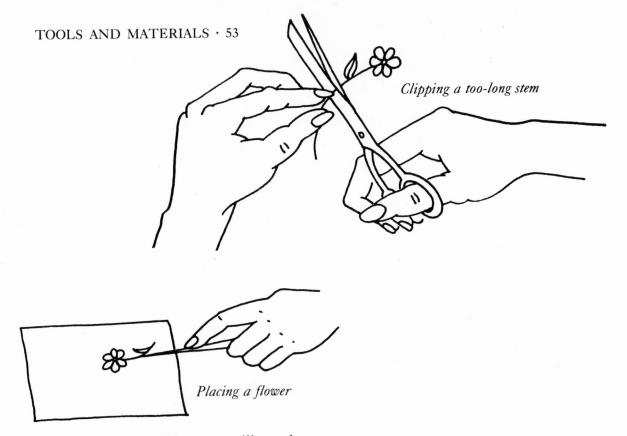

Clipping a too-long stem

Placing a flower

For color washing you will need:

A box of dime-store paints
Three brushes:
  #2 brush for painting
  #2 brush to use as dry brush
  another small brush in case you use too much color
    and want to remove some of it. (If a brush comes
    with your paint box you can use it for this pur-
    pose.)
A small glass or jar of water
A small jar of white poster paint, which is rather thick
  and must be diluted.
A roll of paper towels
And, of course, your tweezers for lifting and your thin
  tool for pushing.

You can mix your paints on the back of your paint box. For example, if you want a lighter shade of rose, put some red on the back of the box and mix a little white poster paint with it until you get the shade you want. A piece of glass can also be used for mixing.

If you find you like color washing, and I hope you do, you may want to invest in better watercolors and more expensive brushes.

I used my dime-store paints for years. Then Glory suggested that I try Windsor & Newton artists' watercolors. Many of these are permanent and a pleasure to work with. The Windsor & Newton brushes are a pleasure to use, too. One word of caution—always keep your brushes scrupulously clean and store them standing up in a jar. These watercolors and brushes are expensive, but they will last for a long time. To start with, however, the cheaper paints will serve the purpose.

The Chinese white in the more expensive watercolors is excellent. The white in the cheaper watercolors does not seem to do a good job and that is why I used white poster paint, which I still like, but the Chinese white is better.

I also found a little metal pan with six indentations, which is just made for mixing colors. It cost me 55¢ and I think can be found in any store that sells watercolors.

I color wash my flowers on paper kitchen towels. I fold one towel in half and then in half again. This makes a sort of cushion to work on, and as you paint your flowers you can run your brush onto it and it will absorb excess paint. I keep changing sides as it gets dirty. I use the corners for wiping excess water from my brush. I think you will find this method very convenient.

If you want to do a super job of color washing and you don't mind using your time and patience to the utmost, try using a magnifying glass while color washing. This shows you exactly how much color you are using. Hold the magnifying glass in your left hand and brush with your right hand. Keep your dry brush handy to use immediately.

This is the procedure I use in color washing. I decide what color to use. If I want a darker or lighter shade I mix it until it is the shade I want. With a damp brush, never wet so that it is dripping, I brush color lightly on the flower, keeping my brush sideways, and then onto the paper toweling. I brush immediately with my dry brush. This seems to set the color without distorting it. Always do this lightly.

After all your flowers, stems, and leaves are color washed, go over the picture a little at a time and be sure everything is in place and exactly the way you want it to be. Now you are ready to glue. For this I use white glue. You will also need your tweezers, sharp tool, and a nail file. I have found that if I use the pointed tool for lifting and dip

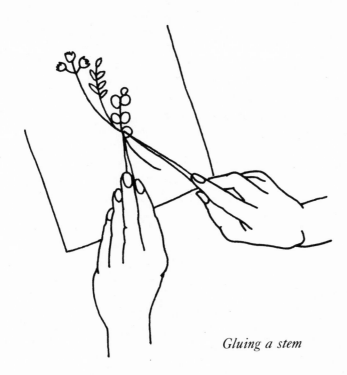

Gluing a stem

my nail file gently in the glue I can slip it easily and quickly where I want it to be. I put a glob of glue on a piece of cardboard so that I can control just how much glue to use. I only use a speck because it is not necessary to use much and a big glob would show. If you are careful and use only a small amount, no one will ever know you have glued. The glue dries transparent and becomes invisible. The nail file seems to be the best tool for slipping the glue under the flower, leaf, or stem because it is flat and slips under things easily. I do not use the tweezers when gluing, but I always keep them handy because sometimes a flower will slip, and the tweezers are the best instrument to use to put it back in its place.

These are the only tools you will need to create a flower picture, to color wash, and then glue it. After this is done the picture will be ready for framing.

Never rush any stage of developing your picture to its completion. Every stage contributes to the final success of your painting—the pressing, the arranging of your material, the color washing, the gluing, and finally the framing.

Step-by-Step: Reprise

Here are the stages, simply put:

1. Select frame and background—glue velvet or whatever background material you decide to use on cardboard cut to fit frame.
2. Create your flower painting.
3. Color wash your flowers if you decide to do so.
4. Set aside for at least an hour.
5. Glue.
6. Set aside overnight if possible.
7. Wash glass for frame until it is sparkling clean, and make sure the background is spotless.
8. Put glass on picture—complete backing—sign your name and date proudly on the back of your lovely, original painting.

*Flower pictures and teapots
just seem to go together.*

Creative Pressing

The ultimate success of your dried flower painting depends a great deal on how careful you have been in pressing your material. It is really important to pick flowers at the right time, too, and to press them immediately, with imagination and care. They will be flexible at the time of picking, and you can arrange and curve them so that they press in graceful lines for which you will be thankful when the time comes to create your painting.

I did not realize the importance of creative pressing when I first began pressing flowers. My first mistake was pressing them between paper towels. They pressed well, but the design of the paper came off on the flowers and made them look quilted. Later in this chapter I will tell you what I use now. Then, too, I did not always arrange them carefully and too many became distorted in the pressing.

Remember that what you are doing when you press green living plants is drawing all the moisture from them. They are full of moisture when first picked and are therefore easy to change at this time, but once the moisture has been drained from them, they are set forevermore. This is why they should be picked on a dry day—the drier they are to start with the better they will press. If they are picked with the dew or rain on them they will not press well and will turn brown. It is possible to press a flower that is damp when picked, if you dry it thoroughly with a cleansing tissue, but you must be sure it is completely dry.

The important thing is to select the proper paper for pressing your material. I first tried paper towels, then newspaper, but after I discovered manila paper I never used paper towels or newspaper again. Paper towels have a textured design in them, which comes off on the flowers. Cleansing tissues are absorbent but too thin. Manila paper is absorbent and has no design texture—it is also the most convenient size. I always use manila drawing paper for the flowers I grow at home. When I take walks with my family looking for material I take along some copies of *Organic Gardening.* It is a small magazine and fits easily into a purse, and the paper is very absorbent and not unlike newspaper. I let whatever I have picked dry in these papers and then I transfer the material to manila paper. Telephone books and pads of newsprint paper that can be bought in art stores are both good, and I have used them at times, but I feel that manila paper is more absorbent. The way my flowers look when they have finished drying proves this to me. I like manila paper for another reason, too. It comes in a very convenient size—9″ × 12″. It fits well in most magazines and large books, while newspaper has to be cut to size. Also, manila paper is a creamy color and the flowers you are pressing look good on it. (See Color Plate 1) Perhaps this is not important, but it gives me aesthetic pleasure. Flow-

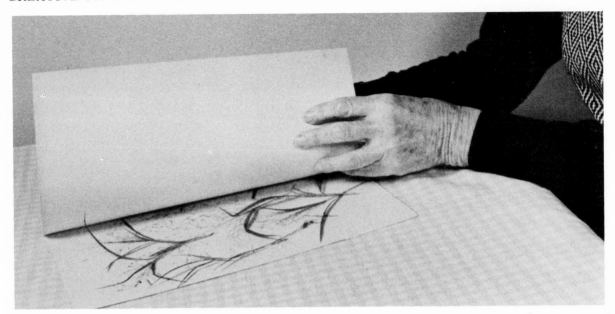

Use a gentle, rolling motion when you place a sheet of manila paper over the sheet on which you've placed your flowers for pressing.

ers pressed this way come out looking natural, full of color, and they stay that way. You can also use manila paper to store your finished flowers. I keep these sheets full of material in piles about ten inches high, and in darkness whenever possible.

I usually gather about a dozen flowers for pressing at a time. I lay the flowers neatly on a piece of manila paper, arranging them the way I want them to look when they are dry. Do not crowd the flowers or let them touch. Press each into shape gently but firmly. Then carefully place another sheet of manila paper over the first sheet. Hold it firmly on the left side and roll the sheet gently over the flowers to the right. Use a rolling motion to do this. Then put sheets in a large book or magazine, place in a dark, dry place, and put a heavy weight on the book. I use an old-fashioned flatiron plus a large heavy book, but just the heavy book will do as well.

Leave them like this for at least a week—it will not hurt to leave them longer than this, but if you are in a hurry to get them pressed check after a week's time. Try to wait a week because if you look at them too soon and they are still damp you may ruin them. I know, because when I first began pressing flowers my curiosity got the better of me, I looked too soon, and the flowers crumbled. So leave them at least a week, and if they are still not quite dry, leave them a few days more.

How will you know when they are dry enough? Lift the paper gingerly and examine them. You can generally tell by looking at them—they will look dry. If you are in doubt feel them. If they are not quite dry they will not lift readily from the paper, and you will feel a slight moisture in them. If this happens, close the paper and leave undisturbed for at least three days more.

It will not take long before you find yourself becoming very adept at adjusting the flowers, stems, and leaves into the positions you wish them to assume permanently. One of the secrets is to learn how to gently roll the paper over them without disturbing them.

Do not become discouraged if a flower does become distorted. If it has a good color, keep it. You may be able to use it peeking around another flower when you are layering your material to give an impression of depth. I hardly ever throw anything away, because I have found that I can always find a use for everything eventually.

However if you want your finished pictures to be consistently good you must press carefully and with imagination. Place each flower, stem, and leaf as carefully and prettily as you possibly can, roll the top sheet of paper over them gently with care and you will be rewarded 99 percent of the time with beautifully pressed flowers.

Try to press a few flowers, leaves, and stems every sunny day. There is no such thing as having too much

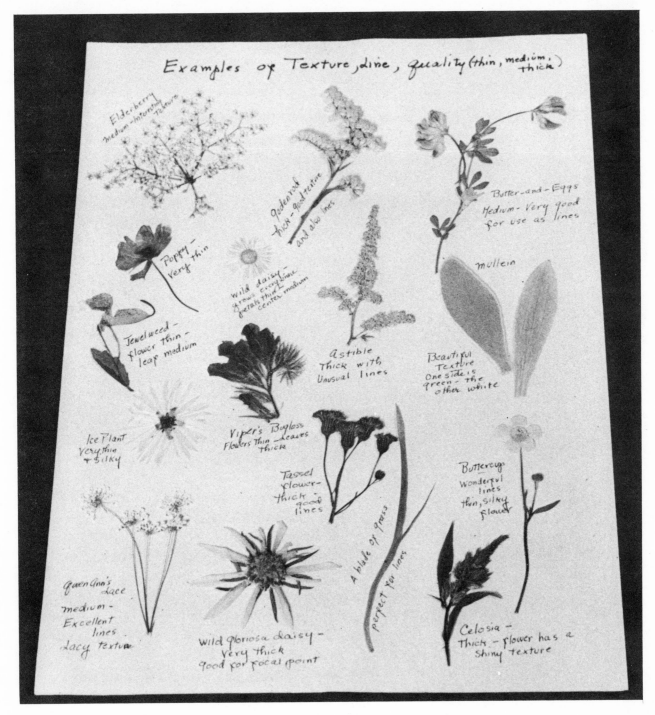

Your pressing sheets can be delightful resources. This one is labeled to show you examples of different texture and line qualities.

material. The more variety you have the more you will have to choose from when the time comes for you to start creating your paintings. It is true you can create pictures with a limited amount of material, but you will be limited by the amount of material you have to choose from. It is such a joy to have stacks of drying papers full of colorful, graceful flowers, stems, and leaves to work with. (See Color Plate 1.)

Before I go any further, I should tell you to check your stored flowers once in a while to see if any bugs have appeared. One year I found some tiny little things eating away. How they lived like that, pressed down and in the dark I don't know. I quickly went through all my piles of pressing papers and eliminated them. Now I put moth balls where I store my pressing papers and this seems to have solved the problem. I have never seen any since, but I still check.

Another thing to remember is that it is sometimes necessary to cut and trim your flowers, stems, and leaves as you are arranging them on your pressing paper. Heavy stems should be cut away; so should any flowers or leaves that do not have a definite form or ones that overlap and hide each other. If leaves are in the wrong place do not hesitate to cut them, dry them separately, and, when it comes time to arrange them, use them to their best advantage. When arranging your pictures, place every flower, leaf, and stem so that it will show to its best advantage.

Curve your stems whenever you can—coax them into the lines you want. And remember, most flowers and leaves have a right and wrong side. Be careful of this—if you have the wrong side up, it will be just as noticeable as a dress made with a combination of right and wrong sides showing.

Take a little extra time and care and press creatively. If you have lots of beautiful, colorful flowers carefully pressed and ready to use you cannot help but succeed in creating a lovely, original, one-of-a-kind flower painting.

Color Plate 1 Pressing sheets with scissors and tools for lifting and placing. *Left:* golden glow, field daisies, black-eyed-Susan vine flower, maple leaf, coreopsis, borage flower, larkspur, butter-and-eggs, poppy, violas, evening primrose, candytuft, dusty miller, coriander, grasses, and weeds. *Center:* geranium, columbine, Queen Anne's lace, evening Lychnis, violas, sedum, apple blossoms, elderberry flower, jewel weed, potentilla, cherry blossoms, hosta leaf, larkspur, candytuft, two forms of dusty miller. *Right:* marigold, phlox, asparagus fern, blue and pink sage, a snapdragon spray, coralbells, a pink, a viola, an evening primrose, celosia (crested type), columbine, cosmos, grass, celosia (plume type), buttercup, viola and okra leaf.

Color Plate 2   Bottom left: viper's bugloss, elderberry flowers, butter-and-eggs, violas, Queen Anne's lace, emilia, and lupin. *Bottom right:* spray of cloud grass with a viola; butter-and-eggs at base; two jewelweed flowers; above purple viola in center is a spray of blue sage; a pink is at center top with a small marigold blossom. *Middle left:* base of coreopsis; butter-and-egg sprays; three delphinium. *Middle right:* focal point is a leontopdium with Queen Anne's lace; above, a spray from a shadblow tree, pink larkspur and buds, a viola, and two spears of grass. *Top:* raspberry leaf at base; above, grass and pink and purple larkspur; a few circles of Queen Anne's lace.

Color Plate 3   This shows what can be done with two colors—yellow and white. The focal point is two yellow hosta leaves with a circle of Queen Anne's lace. From this are sprays of Queen Anne's lace, a tall spike of grass, some orange blossom flowers, grasses, buds of larkspur, baby's breath, and more Queen Anne's lace.

Color Plate 4   At the top of the picture in the middle is the leaf of a flowering cabbage, and on it three petals the name of which I do not remember. The focal point is three chrysanthemums, leaves of the snow-on-the-mountain, one potentilla blossom, elderberry flowers and florets of white larkspur. To the right, a spray of larkspur buds on a leaf of coleus, and an anemone blanda flower. On the right is a leaf of a sweet potato vine, with a viola on it and one to the right of it. Above these are ferns and weeds with florets of Queen Anne's lace; running through the middle, a black-eyed-Susan vine on which are hydrangea florets. At top on right is a blue lace flower and a made-up flower of the leaves of the black-eyed-Susan vine and tillandsia flowers. Also a blue lace flower, grasses, Queen Anne's lace florets, a fuschia, and clarkia flower.

Color Plate 5 This is a favorite of mine. I love the combination of red and white and black with a touch of green. The focal point is two larkspur flowers with buds, Queen Anne's lace, scarlet sage, and coral bells. A scarlet sage blooms above cloud grass, a white larkspur from the maidenhair fern and from this are some drooping begonia blossoms.

Color Plate 6   I love working with ovals.
    The focal point is three larkspur, with field daisies with a spray of
Queen Anne's lace, larkspur through the center, circles of Queen Anne's
lace, and sweet peas around the edge of the bouquet.

Color Plate 7 Glory's favorite picture. She likes the graceful lines of the grasses with larkspur forming the center line and side lines. The focal point is made up of larkspur, with a pink on each side of leaves from a nandina plant I grew in Maryland.

Color Plate 8   These two pictures show what I mean by getting a
three-dimensional effect, especially the one on the right. *Left:* focal point of
two hosta leaves and a spray of delphinium leaves in between; from this is a
large spray of larkspur, and a combination of goldenrod, daisies, Queen
Anne's lace, violas, celosia, coreopsis, butter and eggs; flower above the
hosta leaf on the right is a bachelor's button. *Right:* focal point of one
bergamot flower and leaf; from this are Queen Anne's lace, larkspur,
bachelor's button, more bergamot flowers, violas, snapdragon, coreopsis,
and candytuft.

Step-by-Step: Reprise

1. Pick your material on a dry, sunny day.
2. Gather only as much material as you can conveniently press.
3. Place each flower, leaf, and stem on manila paper. Keep them separated—never let them touch—or they will dry together and be ruined.
4. As you place each one, press it gently against the paper in the position you wish.
5. Gently roll another sheet of manila paper over them, trying not to disturb their positions.
6. Place sheets in pressing book.
7. Place a heavy book on top of your pressing book, and, if you have one, a flatiron on top of this—a heavy rock will also be good.
8. Leave undisturbed at least one week. If flowers are very thick, leave them for at least two weeks.
9. Check your pressing sheets after this time to see if they are dry.
10. If they are dry, place the sheets in your stockpile, ready for using.

As you may have guessed, I love a touch of the Orient. These plants are growing in a Japanese hibachi.

4
Backgrounds and Colors

I have tried many different backgrounds for my pictures—rice paper, black emory cloth, tan sandpaper, silk, satin, grass matting, taffeta, burlap, felt, and velvet. After trying all these I always come back to velvet. It makes such a rich backdrop for flowers, it has a kind of Victorian feeling that goes well with pressed flower pictures, all flowers and foliage look lovely against it, and they cling to it enough so that it helps to keep them in place. Silks and satins are slippery; flowers slide all over the place on them and drive you crazy. The other materials can be interesting but they do not give the rich effect of velvet. Burlap is a good background for the thicker types of flowers and can be very striking, but flowers cling to it too much and this makes it hard to get them off when you want

75

to move them. There is a paper on the market that has a velvety finish, and the back can be peeled off like shelving paper. It is called velour paper, and most hardware stores carry it. It comes in black, green, and other colors. It is easier to apply to cardboard than velvet is, since velvet has to be cut to fit the frame with some overlapping and gluing. Next to velvet I like this paper best, but it still does not give the glow and richness of velvet.

I was lucky in so many ways when I began my new hobby. I had a lot of antique velvets, which my mother had kept in a trunk in the attic for years. Thank goodness, she could never throw anything away. These antique velvets have beautiful colors, and they have a quality you do not find in modern velvets. They glow and change as you look at them, and they look different in different lights. Look for old velvet dresses and drapes at flea markets, garage sales, and church sales.

I have tried all the colors of the rainbow, too. After trying them all, I have decided I like black, brown, dark and light green, deep purple, dark gold, and delft blue the best.

I love black velvet with gold frames trimmed with a touch of black, or with white frames or black and white frames, or plain gold. Dark brown looks wonderful with maple frames, light brown with dark wood frames. If you can find any frames with a touch of blue then blue velvet looks stunning, and it also looks elegant with old gold frames. Deep purple and plum both look black until you throw a light on them, then the purple shows up and looks very rich. Dark green velvet is a wonderful background for all flowers because it is like the green of the earth. Light green looks good with dark green stems and leaves. Dark gold and pale yellow are pretty, but not all flowers look good with these colors. They both seem to need blue and lavender flowers and certain shades of green—you will have to experiment.

The colors I have had trouble with are beige, red, lavender, white, orange, and gray. Not many flowers seem to look their best against these colors, at least not for me. I have made some pictures with a beige background, which turned out well, but it took a long time to find the right combination.

You can use beige, white, or pale gray to create unusual pictures using only flowers, stems, and leaves that have turned brown or black. The tiny flowers of the butter-and-eggs wild flower will sometimes turn jet black and are lovely. The small young tips of the sumac tree and the herb bedstraw will always turn black, but butter-and-eggs can be unpredictable. If you want to try this, save the ones that turn black until you have enough for a picture.

You will have to keep experimenting with different backgrounds and colors to find out which you like the best. What may be best for me may not be best for you. I am sure any color may be used if you can find the right combination to make it come alive.

This matter of color and backgrounds depends upon individual taste. Some people love purple, others love red, others blue, and so on. I love all colors and try to use them all—it's just a matter of using them the right way.

In a fresh flower arrangement, the container used helps create a certain effect. In dried flower pictures, the frame can do much the same thing. The frame you choose will be your container, and can add a great deal to the beauty of your work.

In Chapter 9, "Frames and Framing," which was written by my husband Frank, you'll find out how to assemble—and disassemble—various kinds of frames. I love old frames—rarely do you find two exactly alike. Somehow, dried flowers look their best in old frames. Perhaps this is because flower pressing and arranging is an ancient art, lost for a time and now coming again into its own.

I have—or rather, Frank has—used large frames, medium frames, and small frames for my pressed flower pictures. I like the medium-sized ones best, but that does not keep us from trying others. Tiny oval frames can frame graceful, dainty flowers, and large frames can frame large flowers with bold foliage, which will make beautiful and striking pictures.

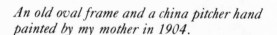

An old oval frame and a china pitcher hand painted by my mother in 1904.

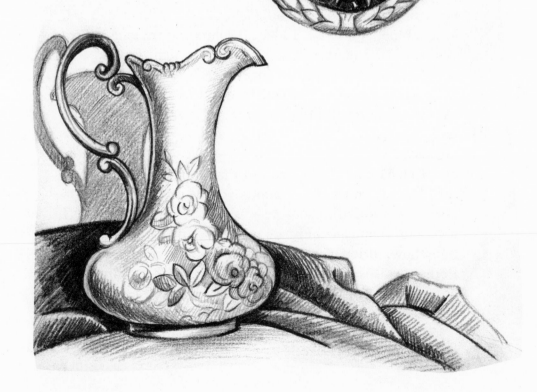

Good frames are expensive these days, sometimes prohibitively so. Even plastic frames have become ridiculously high. So I go out looking for my favorite old frames. Everywhere I go I look for frames—at garage sales, flea markets, church bazaars—they may be found just about anywhere. And my friends and relatives are out there looking for me, too. Collecting frames can be a hobby in itself.

The combination of this graceful frame and equally graceful figure gives me a sense of more leisurely times gone by.

Bunny tails and layered, overlapping flowers and grasses create a three-dimensional effect here.

5
Rules of
the Game

The talented people who create fresh flower arrangements have certain rules they usually follow, but I have read that they do not hesitate to break them and, in so doing, often create something unique and outstanding. Some of these rules may also be used in making pressed flower pictures, but you too may break them if you so desire. I think someone once said that rules are made to be broken, so do not follow the ones I am going to give you too closely. You can make your own rules with pressed flower pictures.

A pressed flower picture can be created in much the same way you would create a fresh flower arrangement. You first establish a line and then fill in around it with flowers and leaves.

The Japanese were the first to make rules about flower arranging, and this is as it should be because flower arranging is for them a way of life. Their rules can be very helpful to you especially if you are a beginner.

The Japanese have a very simple way of establishing a line in fresh flower arrangements, and you can use the same principles in pressed flower pictures. They start with three lines—the lines of Heaven, Earth, and Man.

The longest line is the Heaven line, which rises above the other two. The second in height is the Man line. The shortest is the Earth line. These lines can guide you and help you to get started. Once you have established these three lines you can fill them in, in any way you wish. All lines extend from the Heaven line, which is the dominant line; the Man line gives strength, and the Earth line gives balance. In the center of these three lines you will establish your focal point. This will be the center of interest to balance the whole, and you will create your arrangement around it. One beautiful, well-pressed flower, a few leaves, or a fan of Queen Anne's lace can be the starting point for your picture. If you have three curving, graceful lines and a focal point to start with, you will find it a great help in creating your painting. Try using grass for your lines—it has wonderful curves and looks like it is blowing in the wind.

When you are arranging fresh flowers, you first put in two or three sprays to give a line and framework, and then you start adding flowers to fill it out and make a complete arrangement. Here's a trick to borrow from fresh flower arrangers—if you cannot find the right flower for a certain spot put any flower of the size you need there temporarily and then change it when you find the perfect one. This is exactly what you do in a pressed flower painting. And, while you are doing this, keep the whole arrangement in proportion. Just as you would not use peonies in a little vase or pinks in a huge vase, you would not use flowers or foliage too large or too small for the frame you are working

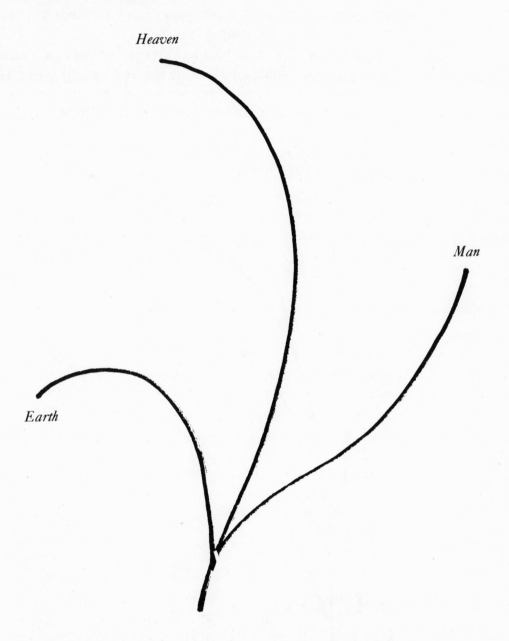

Heaven

Man

Earth

The basic heaven, man, and earth lines that Orientals have always used in flower arranging.

with. It is merely a matter of having a good eye for balance, contrast, line, and color, and this can be learned. You will be surprised at how simple it is.

I do not think you have to worry about lines too much. It is only when you are beginning that it may help you to be aware of them. Actually each stem and spray you use will assume its own line, and nature has a way of being graceful

A basic curve established with grass and ferns, with flowers and leaves branching off. See also color plate 5.

and right. Many flowers may be picked with stems to help you achieve your effects. Queen Anne's lace is an excellent one for this purpose. If you pick and press some sprays of snapdragons with leaves and then press some of the blossoms separately, they will also be graceful and useful. Baby's breath, bladder campion, and coral bells may all be used to create lines.

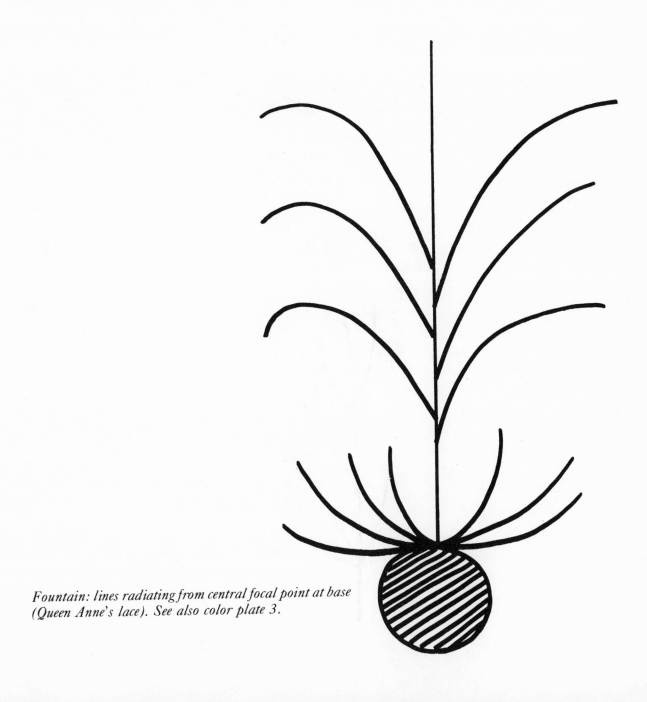

Fountain: lines radiating from central focal point at base (Queen Anne's lace). See also color plate 3.

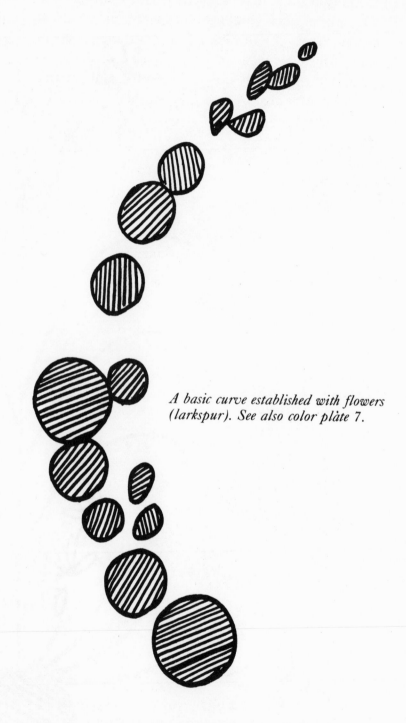

A basic curve established with flowers (larkspur). See also color plate 7.

Two arcs established by flower color (yellow buttercups and white shadblow blossoms). See also color plate 10 (oval).

An example of symmetry with many triads established by flower groups. See also color plate 4.

Bouquet: rounded lines at base established by Queen Anne's lace with flowers filling out the bouquet. See also color plate 6.

Texture is a subtle element in pressed flower pictures. I did not become aware of this all at once. It took a period of time for me to realize how very different flower textures can be. Some flowers such as poppies and the evening primrose come out of the pressing sheets looking, feeling, and shining like silk. Sprays of elderberry have a rough texture and almost look like a rough material. Each flower and leaf has its own particular texture, as you will see when you begin to examine them. I believe that blended flower textures help to give a picture that certain something extra you are striving for. You may not even be aware of it but the effect is there.

When you have created a picture that you especially like, look at it carefully. Unconsciously you have often used a combination of light and dark, smooth and rough, dull and shiny, round and pointed. Not everything at once, maybe, but some of these elements are there.

Color is the element that perhaps everyone responds to the most in a pressed flower picture. Luckily almost all flower colors blend together. There may be times when you want to create a picture for a room with a special color scheme. In a yellow room shades of yellow and orange and some contrasting color such as red or purple or blue can be the center of the whole room. A pink bedroom looks lovely with pictures of pink and red and lavender flowers with touches of green and white.

Color, contrast, and texture used effectively can produce unusual and beautiful flower pictures. If you can find some flower paintings by the Flemish painters you will see how they used every color and every texture and the result is gorgeous. Every picture will be a new experience, and it is exciting to see what you can do with it.

There is still another way to achieve unusual effect in your pictures. You can sometimes get a three-dimensional effect by layering and overlapping your flowers. This must

Maple Leaves

Envied by us all
   turning to such loveliness—
      red leaves that fall.

SHIKO

be done with discretion because if overdone the effect is messy. This three-dimensional effect seems to happen often by accident. I keep striving for it, and it eludes me, and then suddenly it happens. (See Color Plates 8 and 12). Overlap flowers as they grow in the border, have them peeking around leaves, place some flowers over others.

Another important thing to remember is the importance of contour and form. A pressed flower painting needs a contrast of shapes to bring it to life. A mixture of round forms such as daisies and larkspur will instantly begin to take on the character of a painting when spike forms such as grasses and the spike form of blue sage are added.

I know that in the beginning all these things I am telling you will seem strange if you have never thought of them before, but, please believe me, it will only take the making of two or three pictures to show you how easy these rules are, and you won't even think of them after a short time because they will have become a part of you.

The Red Peony

It falls, the peony—
  and upon each other lie
    petals, two or three.

BUSON

Creating a
Flower Painting

6

When you feel you have enough material to work with, and you have chosen a frame and prepared the background, it is time to sit down and create a flower painting.

Put a pile of pressing papers containing your material on your working surface next to your frame. Gather your tools for lifting and placing. What you are going to do now is virtually paint a picture with flowers.

Start paging through your manila sheets filled with the colorful and graceful material you have gathered and pressed. I start by establishing my center of interest, which is the starting point. Sometimes I use leaves, sometimes a large beautiful flower, very often a fan of Queen Anne's lace. Another effect that is lovely when it can be achieved is the feeling of little plants growing on the forest floor.

On the following pages you'll find five step-by-step drawings showing you how this flower painting was assembled. Try using it as a pattern if you want some practice before creating your own flower paintings.

Small grasses and tiny leaves will create this earthy base from which your flowers can grow.

I am looking at some of the centers of interest I have used. One has a small bunch of elderberry flowers with a few leaves of viper's bugloss on each side. Another has two leaves of velvety mullein with a single flower of wild bergamot in the center, which for some reason looks like a water lily. In another, I chose a large fan of Queen Anne's lace with daisies, bunny tails, butter-and-eggs, and pansies in sprays above it. Yet another has two small circles of Queen Anne's lace with a blue and white larkspur in the center. Another has two plaintain leaves, which turned a pretty yellow with pressing, a circle of Queen Anne's lace in the center with a large fan of Queen Anne's lace springing from it. I could go on indefinitely. The choice is endless.

From this center of interest you now start selecting sprays, stems, or grasses with curving lines to give you an

A

Creating the focal point with celosia in front of Queen Anne's lace and larkspur on either side.

outline to work with. There are many different forms this outline may take. These are described in the preceding chapter.

Once your outline is established, start experimenting. Select flowers, leaves, buds and sprays that look as though they are blooming and growing on your outline. You will

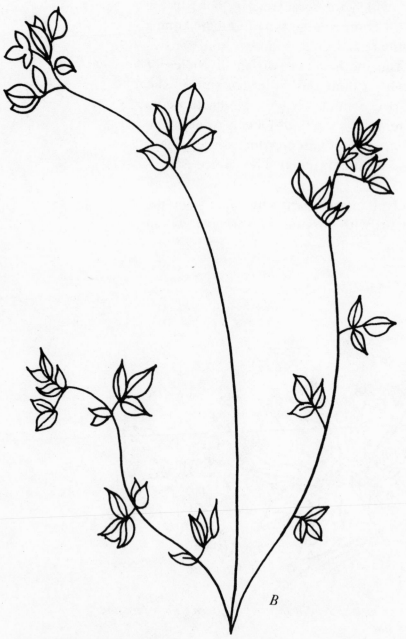

Establishing basic lines—heaven, earth, man—with stems that flower from focal point.

soon learn how to do this. Place and replace all sorts of flowers and leaves at first. If they do not look right to you put them back on the pressing paper and keep trying new ones.

These are some of the things I do while trying to create a painting. I move the flowers around. I put the

Filling out basic lines with grasses.

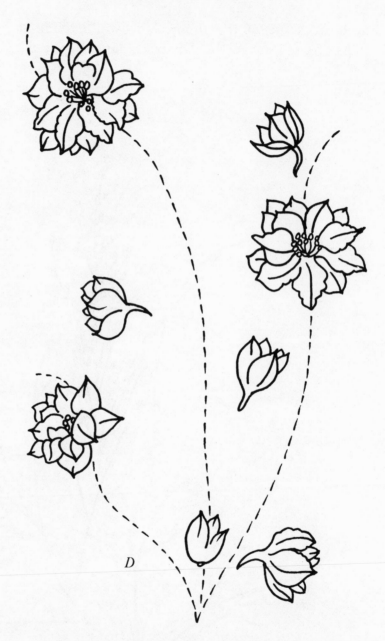

Placing flowers and buds at strategic point (larkspur).

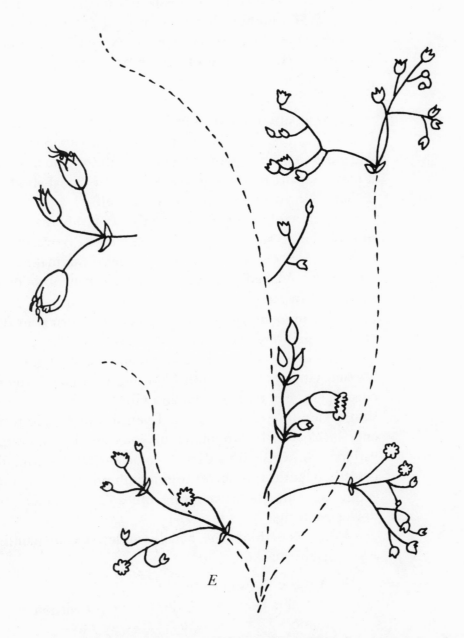

Finishing touch created by smaller flowers in empty spaces (baby's breath and bladder campion).

Trace each outline in sequence—A-B-C-D-E—and you will have the finished black-and-white picture in line form.

flowers on the bottom of the picture on the top. I try changing sprays from the right-hand side to the left or vice versa—very often they will look better that way. I keep trying. When nothing seems to work, I get a fresh pile of pressing papers and start over again. Nine times out of ten this works. This is one of the things that makes flower painting so fascinating—at any turn of the page you may create a masterpiece.

People often ask me how long it takes to do a painting. It is impossible to answer this question. Sometimes you will create a perfect painting in a short time. The next time it may take any number of trys before you are satisfied with it. Set your own pace and enjoy yourself.

When working on a painting that is stubborn, it sometimes helps to stand away from it—move a flower here, a stem there. One line added or taken away can make such a difference. A small curving line or a touch of color can suddenly turn an ordinary picture into a painting.

Curving lines and the right colors will turn your flowers into a painting. Color can make it seem as though it has just been picked out of the garden, and makes it glow with life and vitality. By carefully choosing your colors you can create paintings that are rich and vibrant, others that are a subtle blending of soft colors. Even if you decide to use only black and brown material, you can, by choosing a variety of browns with a dash of color, make a painting that is softly beautiful. A secret to remember is that very often yellow or white helps to bring life and excitement to a flower painting.

When you think you have completed your painting, ask yourself these questions.

1. Are the lines graceful?
2. Are the flowers and leaves in proportion to the frame?
3. Do colors contrast and blend?

4. Do you have a variety of textures to create interest?
5. Does your painting look natural and unforced?
6. If you had intended to give it to someone as a present, do you feel as though you want to keep it for yourself?

The answer to all of these should be "yes," of course. If it is not then keep working.

Just as in fresh flower arrangements, one must learn to capture a bit of nature in a vignette. That is why it is so important to study and observe intently the world around you, and watch how nature creates beauty in so many ways—form, textures, colors, balance, moods, and in an everchanging way. You too will use your material in everchanging ways, because no two flowers, leaves, or stems will ever be exactly the same. You can even create your own exotic combinations. You do not have to put pansy leaves with pansies. Instead you may use any kind of leaf that looks well, provided the final effect is believable and natural.

A pressed flower picture is in effect a collage. You take a flower here, a stem there, and you fashion with the materials nature has given you, a painting. It is the way you put the material together that makes the difference.

Tillandsia + Black-eyed-Susan vine = "new flower"
See also color plate 4, top right-hand corner.

I should tell you that on the day I am going to work with my pressed flowers I make sure the dishes are washed, the beds made, the house neat, and dinner cooking slowly. If I did not do these everyday things first they probably would not get done. Once I begin working on a pressed flower painting, time goes by, and I forget everything else.

While I am working, these are the ideals I strive for: simplicity without bareness, a flowing line, appealing color combinations, a natural effect, an attempt to capture a vignette of the glory of past gardens to keep forever within the confines of a frame.

So never become discouraged. Keep working until you create a painting that will always revive the memories of your garden on a warm, sunny day, with the sun shining, birds singing, flowers blooming. Keep working and changing until suddenly you see the painting you want. You will know when you have finally achieved the effect you are trying to create. You will put together an arrangement of flowers, stems and leaves that will delight you and you will know "This is it."

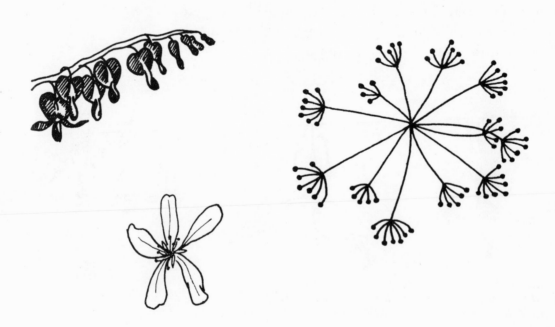

Step-by-Step: Reprise

These are the things to remember.

1. You should have a focal point as a center of interest and the starting point from which the painting will grow. It should not be too eye-catching but should blend in with the overall effect.

2. Have lines flowing from the focal point.

3. Strive for simplicity and graceful lines.

4. Too much going on can distract the eye and give a messy effect, and yet you will need plenty of material to furnish interest and avoid a feeling of bareness.

5. Do not "plunk" material and leave it there. Keep moving it around until you find the perfect spot for it.

6. Keep your material well centered. I have to be careful of this. For some reason my flowers want to go to the left.

7. Try for asymmetrical balance rather than a perfect balance, because this always creates a more interesting picture. Of course, there are exceptions to this.

*Another combination of a pressed flower
picture with Oriental artifacts.*

7

A Touch
of Magic:
Color Washing

You have created your pressed flower painting. It is lovely, and you should be proud of it.
There is yet another step to complete if you want to keep it forever just as it is now.

It took a lot of time and patience to get to this point. If you grew your own flowers you had to plant the seeds, care for and tend the plants until they blossomed, and pick and press the flowers, stems, and leaves. If you did not grow your own material you went looking for it, and this too took time and effort. Then you had to choose a frame and prepare the background before you could create your painting, and of course this was the climax of all your preparation. Why not go a step further and take precautions to keep this painting always as it is today.

You can do this by the step I call color washing. Color washing is the application of a thin film of color applied

105

with a feather touch. I have read books on pressed flower pictures that say you should not paint flowers, and I agree. Unless you can use a color wash and have it look natural you should leave the flowers as they are. If, however, you can use a film of color so delicate that it does not change in the slightest the color of the flower, it will make them look as natural as the day you picked them, and they will stay that way.

Before you color wash study each flower and leaf. Treat each one as an individual problem. Sometimes it is best to color wash only the back of a flower. I do this with buttercups. Color washing the front would ruin their marvelous glow and sheen. The color on the back does not show through, but it seems to help them remain yellow—it fades a little but not completely.

If any stems need shortening do it at this time. Then with loving care apply the color wash as lightly as possible. Do this on your folded paper towel or manila paper. Have your brush almost dry, and run the color off sideways onto the paper. After you have finished, brush lightly with a dry brush. Each flower and leaf should get your entire attention. Each one is important for the final effect.

Work lightly and quickly. Keep brushing excess paint off on a paper towel. Keep cleaning your brush. For example, if you are color washing a cosmos, do the center first, wash your brush, then do the petals. Cosmos, by the way, has thin petals, but if you are careful, it is easy to color wash.

There are two ways to proceed with color washing. One way, and the hardest way for a beginner, is to take your painting apart piece by piece.

1. Lay each flower, flower spray, or leaf on a separate piece of manila paper, in approximately the same position as they were and will be in your finished picture. When I first started doing this I was scared. I was afraid I would not

be able to reassemble them as they were, and in fact this did turn out to be a tricky thing to do. You may lose your original design; sometimes in the process you may improve on the original, and sometimes you will not. Being able to control this tendency comes with experience. I can promise you that after you have done this a few times you will no longer be afraid. It is good training, and helps you to observe and learn.

2. After removing the original design to the manila paper, clean the background of your painting thoroughly—it will probably have bits of dried debris on it, especially if it is velvet. It will save you time and trouble to keep your background clean. A tiny speck shows up like a sore thumb on a finished flower picture.

3. Color wash each flower and leaf. As you complete them put them back in their original positions, ready for gluing.

The second way is easier I think, and the one I usually use the most.

1. Leave your painting as it is. Lift each flower one at a time and place it on your folded paper towel as I described in Chapter 2, "Tools and Materials." Color wash it and put it back in place.

2. As you lift the flower, clean the empty space with a small piece of masking tape. You can also use a cotton-tipped stick dipped in water and wiped dry and squeezed, or a small paintbrush dipped in water and wiped with cleansing tissue. I sometimes use all of these things, depending upon the amount of space left to clean. When you have finished, put the blossom back in place, then lift the next one, and so on until all are color washed. Slowly and surely the painting should look slightly brighter, but definitely not painted.

Irene color washing a flower.

HELPFUL HINTS

· Try to match your colors as closely as possible, but if the color is not exactly the same it will not matter. You are not painting, but washing with color. For example, if you are working with three different flowers and all of them are a different shade of yellow you can use the same yellow to color wash all of them. The flowers will retain their own shade; the light cover you put on them will brighten them but not color them. And you do not have to match the green of a leaf with the green of your watercolor. If covered lightly, the leaf will absorb the color you are using and turn it into its own shade of green. Similarly, if you color wash an orange flower—coreopsis is a good example—with yellow, orange will still be the predominant color.

· Someday when you do not have anything else to do you might try taking some flowers out of the pressing papers before they are completely dry, color washing them, and putting them back until the time comes to use them. This is not really necessary, but it is a pleasant feeling to open up your pressing papers and find flowers already color washed ready for use. Flowers do seem to absorb color a little better when they are not too crackling dry, but they do not absorb it to the point that it is necessary to take this step. It is a little tricky, too, because you should do it at the right time, when they are dry but not too dry. I just mention this in case you feel like experimenting someday.

· If you have any extra pieces of glass left over after framing, save them. They make good palettes for mixing watercolors, and you can also put them over flowers that want to curl up after being color washed. Sometimes pansies, daisies, and cosmos do this.

· If you want to lighten a color, add a little white poster paint or Chinese white to it. Mix the paint on the back of your watercolor box or in a little bowl, just as you would when doing a watercolor painting. For example, if you wish to use a pale lavender, mix purple with a small amount of either type of white paint until you get the approximate shade you wish.

· If your flowers and leaves look painted you are not doing it right. For an experiment try this: take two flowers of the same species and color for a test. Color wash one of them and then compare the two. The one you color washed should look a little brighter but not painted.

· Each flower has its own individuality, which you will learn to recognize. Some flowers love to be color washed, others resist it. If they resist, stop! Larkspur responds well to color washing and becomes unbelievably lovelier. Pansies seem to love to get their little faces washed. Almost all leaves take to color washing.

· Thin flowers usually cannot be color washed. When they are too thin they fall apart if you try to color wash them. Even the lightest touch will ruin them, so it is best to leave them as they are; although they will lose some of their color in time, they will retain their silkiness and glow.

Four years ago, I made a picture using only paper-thin flowers. The focal point of this is two satin flowers. They are still a satiny, shell-like pink. The other flowers, poppies, forsythia, and clover stems, have turned brown and cream, but the poppies look like mother-of-pearl when a light shines on them. The background is black emory cloth, and the thin flowers cling to it and look as if they have been painted on it. When we lived in Maryland this picture hung on an east wall. For most of the day it looked rather dull, but toward late afternoon, as the sun was setting, this picture caught the rays of the setting sun and sparkled and glowed with life. It was worth waiting for.

· Flowers and leaves of a medium or heavy thickness, if done very delicately, definitely look better when color washed, and survive the passage of time with a timeless look. I feel that it is well worth the time and effort spent.

I find color washing a very relaxing and enjoyable pastime. The results are magical—a fountain of youth for flowers—so surely it is worth the effort (if it is an effort, which it is not for me). I suppose it does take a certain kind of patience, which you either have or do not have. If you want to skip this step, your flower painting will still look good. Pressed flowers take on soft colors with time. If the line and design are good they will never really grow old. I have seen some pressed flower pictures that were made in Palestine about two hundred years ago.

Play about, do
from grass-leaf to grass-leaf!
Jewels of dew!

RANSETSU

At one of the art shows where I exhibited my pictures a girl came up to me and asked if I would like to see some dried flower pictures that had been valued antiques in her family for generations. Of course I said I would very much like to see them, so she went home and returned with them. They were made up into a little booklet, and on each page was a picture. The girl said that it had been sent home as a present to her family by a great-uncle who was travelling many years ago. They were lovely even though all the stems and flowers had turned brown and the only touch of color was the blue of the larkspur wherever it was used.

Once, I put a picture away because for some reason my husband was unable to finish framing it. When I took it out to start working again I could not remember if I had color washed it or not, and I could not tell by looking at it. My husband remembered that I had color washed it. I consider this successful color washing if even I can't tell.

If you do not want to color wash every painting you create, perhaps you will at least try it with a painting you particularly like, or one you intend to give as a present, or one you intend to sell. If you see for yourself what magic a color wash can perform I believe you will be as entranced with the technique as I am.

Step-by-Step: Reprise

1. Remove the flower or leaf you wish to color wash and place it on a folded paper towel.
2. Decide what color you are going to use. If you want a darker or lighter color than is available in your paints, mix to achieve it.
3. With a feather touch, apply color with a damp, not wet, brush. Use your brush sideways and

run color off onto paper. Keep turning the paper around as you color so that the petals you are color washing will be in front of you.

4. As you finish each petal, brush lightly with your dry brush. This takes up any excess color and maintains a natural effect. If your dry brush gets dirty, wash it and wipe it as dry as possible with cleansing tissues.

5. If you feel the color is too strong, go over petal lightly with a damp but not wet brush, then with a dry brush. This usually works, but if you have really used too much color, blot it with a cleansing tissue. I sometimes use my index finger to brush away excess paint. This works well with grasses—run your finger lightly along them. You will probably only have this problem at first. You will soon learn the right amount of paint to use.

6. If a petal should fall off, put it back together with a speck of glue. Put it aside until the glue is completely dry.

7. Color the center of the flower with the tip of the brush. Of course, you'll keep washing off color you have used as you go on to a new color. A daisy is a good example. Go over daisy petals lightly with white poster paint or Chinese white watercolor. Use brush sideways and brush onto paper. Then color center with yellow, using the tip of the brush.

8. Do this with each flower and leaf one by one. Color wash lightly and carefully, then put them in place.

9. When everything is color washed and arranged, you'll be ready for the final step—gluing.

Gluing

8

I love almost everything about making pressed flower paintings—planting the seeds, tending the plants, picking and pressing the flowers, color washing, and creating a flower painting with the results of my labors—but I do not love gluing. For a long time I used to put it off, and occasionally not even do it, but I do not do this anymore. Now I glue as soon as possible after I have first taken a few precautions, to make sure the gluing will be successful. I have learned to take my time and to be careful. You will find the more you glue the easier it will become. As it does with most things, practice makes perfect.

It is something that I think must be done, and it is really not that hard to do. It is tedious more than anything else, but I sincerely believe it is necessary. Some people skip it, I have heard, but I believe you are taking a chance if you do. When I first began I did skip it. I had read that it was not necessary, and I thought, "Good," but I found out that pressed flowers are slippery and they will move if they are not glued. Not all of them do this, but if just one slips a little your painting is ruined. I learned the hard way and now I glue.

There are secrets to learn about gluing that will help you, and I will tell you about them. If you possibly can, pick a rainy, dreary day for gluing. Since there is nothing else to do you won't mind taking your time and doing a thorough, careful job. It's the getting to it that's hard, you know, like cleaning the refrigerator—once you start it isn't so bad.

HELPFUL HINTS

· When you have your painting arranged exactly the way you want it, sit and stare at it for a while. You may notice a few things here and there that can be improved. If so, make some changes. Then put it aside for at least an hour—overnight if possible. If it still looks good to you in the morning, start gluing, but first check again to make sure that every leaf and flower is in its place before you start. It is much easier to change something now than later after the glue has set. This is why it is so important to go over each section. Push every little stem meticulously in place and do the same with leaves and flowers. Look at everything with the idea of memorizing it so that if anything slips—and it will at times—you will be aware of it and put it back in its proper place. At first you will have trouble, but as you do this more and more you will become an expert, and it will not be long before you will wonder why you were having trouble with it.

· I use my sharp dental tool and a nail file for gluing—the sharp tool for lifting and the nail file with a dab of glue on it to slip under flowers and stems. I keep my tweezers close by in case I need them. The exception to this is thin flowers. Glue will show through thin flowers when it dries, so you want to be very careful to use only a little, and that in the middle of the flower where it will not show. To do this it is easier to lift the flower from the velvet, put a dab of glue in the center, and then replace it. If I use paper as a background as I did in the wedding picture (see page 187), I put the glue on with a small brush. This is possible with paper because you can paint the edges of the flowers with thin glue and it will not show. Incidentally, scraps of cardboard are good for putting glue on, instead of reaching into the jar.

Since I am right-handed I use my left hand for lifting, my right hand for gluing. You only have to use a tiny bit of glue, it doesn't take much. The finished painting will look better if it is not obviously glued. Not all the flowers, leaves, and stems have to be glued, usually only the ones on the outer edge and in the middle of the painting have to be secured. You will soon learn which flowers are strategically placed and must be glued, and which ones you may safely leave unglued.

· If you have to lift a flower to glue it, lift it with your tweezers, put a speck of glue on it, and place it back carefully with the tweezers. Sometimes it helps to hold your finger on an inner flower. This will make the outer flower rise just enough to enable you to slip a dab of glue under it quickly. It doesn't take much to make pressed flowers move. If your picture shifts, don't panic. Slowly and patiently tease everything back into place. Whatever you do, never sneeze in the vicinity of your flower painting.

· There may be a problem when you put a weight on a flower to hold it down until it is completely dry. Sometimes it will stick to the weight. Rather than risk this happening (unless it is very thick, since thick flowers don't stick), I hold the flower down with my nail file and count to ten. If the glue still isn't dry and the flower doesn't stay, I count to ten again.

Step-by-Step: Reprise

Here are the things I think are important to remember when you are gluing:

1. Be sure your painting is just the way you want it to be.
2. Keep the painting in its frame while gluing. Flowers do slip sometimes, and unless you have a definite perimeter, your painting may become lopsided.
3. Use two tools, one to lift the flower and one for gluing—a sharp, thin tool for lifting, a nail file for gluing. I have found a nail file works best because it is flat and slips easily under the material without disturbing it.
4. Put some glue on a plate, or a small block of wood, or a piece of cardboard. Dip your tool in it, and remember to use only a dab. Putting the glue on a plate or whatever you decide to use makes the amount easier to control.
5. Keep turning the section you want to glue toward you. For example, if you are gluing the top of the picture, turn it upside down.
6. Don't hurry. Be calm. If anything slips, gently put it back in place.

7. Be critical while you are gluing. Make sure you are not letting anything slip or get lopsided.

8. When you think you are finished, blow gently. If anything moves, glue it.

9. Let the glue harden overnight if possible. The reason for this is if you frame your picture too soon after gluing a speck may stick to the glass. If you have to raise the glass for any reason, then a flower sticking to it may be ruined.

10. There is a way to hasten the drying process. If you put a piece of Styrofoam on the picture, with a flatiron on top of it or a heavy book, you'll find that glue will not stick to the Styrofoam and the picture will be completely dry in half an hour.

I would never recommend not gluing. As I said, I've tried it, and flowers do slip if the picture is handled roughly—or even, sometimes, for no reason at all. It takes such a small amount of glue and time to ensure keeping your precious painting intact that it is surely worth the effort.

Seed packet

Blooms at their peak

Blooms, stems, leaves
arranged on absorbent paper

Your flower reserves

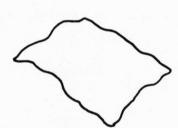

Background material

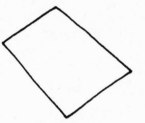

Mounting cardboard

Background material
securely attached to cardboard

Flower arrangement
on velvet background

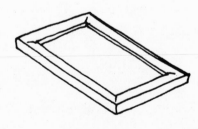

Frame

9

Frames
and Framing

Framing your pressed flower arrangements once you have prepared and secured them on a suitable background is an art in itself; the frame, its glass, and backing material for sealing are all important. The requirements for a successful job of framing are few, but you must follow them carefully in order to protect your creation against dust, moisture, movement, and the effects of atmospheric change. Attractive, permanent framing not only guarantees protection but also serves an artistic purpose by setting off your flower arrangement from any decorative distractions there may be on adjacent wall surfaces.

119

Sources of Frames

Your garden, the roadside, the fields supply you with flowers and interesting leaf sprays. Where do you find your frames? There are three basic sources.

NEIGHBORHOOD SOURCES: OLD FRAMES

Attics, garages, sheds, basements, flea markets, local auctions, friends, and neighbors can be highly productive sources for old frames, generally made of wood. Rarely will frames in this category be without flaws of one kind or another, but they are worth keeping and repairing.

RETAIL STORE OUTLETS: NEW FRAMES

Don't overlook such outlets as dime stores and hardware stores. They often provide you with a variety of frames at reasonable prices. They may be round, oval, rectangular, or square, and made of wood, wood-simulated plastic, or metal. In this category we also include the framing kits that come with instructions for assembly.

WOODWORKING SHOPS: RAW MOLDING LENGTHS

Professional woodworking shops in your area may be able to help you with your frame needs. Such shops cater to exacting requirements for specific pieces of woodwork, and they can turn out raw frame molding to the precise specifications you request.

Old Frames

My object here is to show you how to process or rework old frames. They may be square, rectangular, oval, or round. The width/height proportions may be unusual or awkward by modern standards (Figure 1). In many cases you'll want to cut them down to more appropriate lengths as suggested in the "Recommended Frame Size Proportion Chart." The molding cross sections may be simple or ornate (Figure 2). The finish of the moldings may be one color or several colors (Figure 3). It is important to remember that old wooden frames with interesting moldings are valuable in themselves. If you come across old frames that are close to the right proportions, store them carefully. They are not easy to come by.

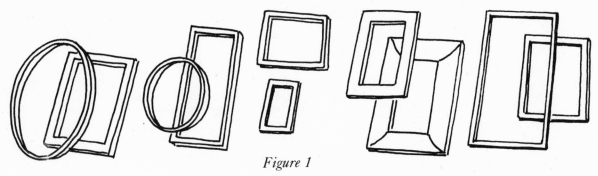

Figure 1

Typical shapes and proportions

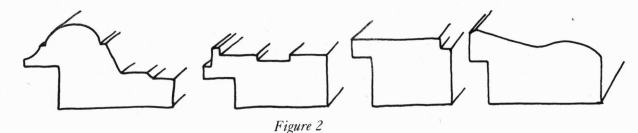

Figure 2

Typical molding cross sections

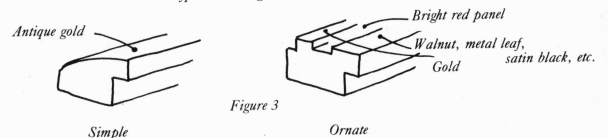

Figure 3

Simple   *Ornate*

Recommended Frame Size Proportion Chart

BASIS FOR CHART:
6″ × 8″ FRAME DIAGONAL

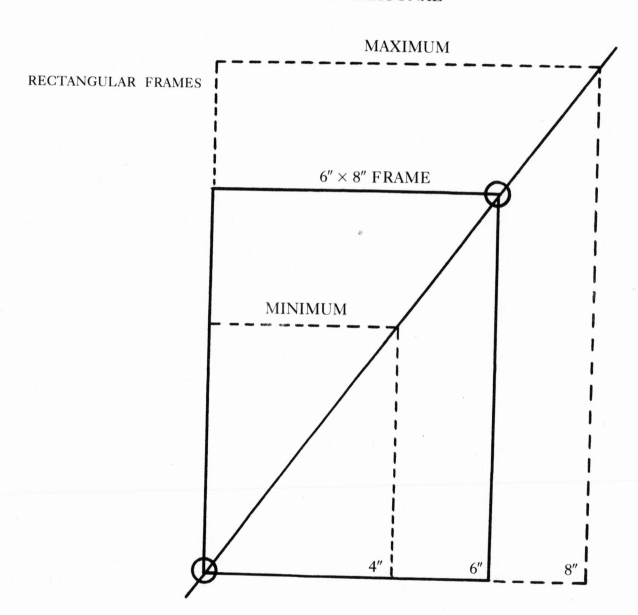

MAXIMUM

RECTANGULAR FRAMES

6″ × 8″ FRAME

MINIMUM

4″   6″   8″

Recommended Maximum Molding Width for Rectangular and Square
Frames:
½ Inch for Minimum Size Frame
1 Inch for Maximum Size Frame

BASIS FOR CHART:
6″ × 6″ FRAME DIAGONAL

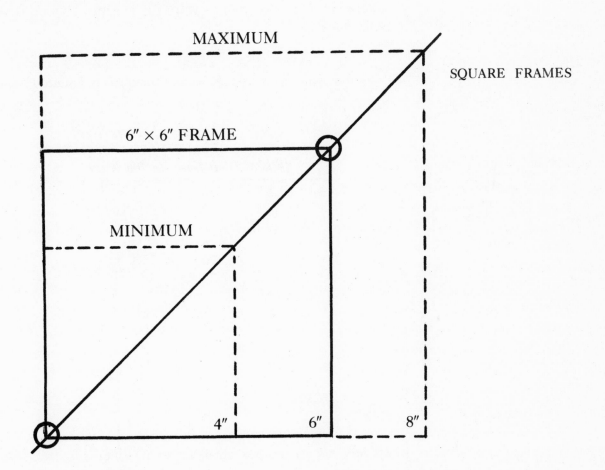

Note:
Both diagrams are shown one-half scale. Redraw them full scale
on a heavy piece of cardboard to serve as a permanent reference.
Then you can put a frame of questionable proportion on your charts
for a proportion check.

Various shapes, cross sections, and molding finishes can be found in just about endless combinations. Choose only those frames that have immediate potential—that is, those that do not need extensive molding repair. Set aside any others for future consideration.

As a basis for writing about old frames, I am going to discuss twelve old wooden frames that I actually converted into usable frames for pressed flower pictures. These twelve overly large frames were turned into sixteen desirable ones.

The following table lists the actual frame sizes I started with.

Table 1 : Original Frame Sizes

Width	Height	Molding Width
8	10	½
9	17	$^{13}/_{16}$
10	12	⅝
12	16	½
12	20	¾
12¾	24	1
14	24	½
15	18½	1½
15¾	24	1⅛
16	18	¾
16	23	1
18	23	¾

If you have a dozen or more old, oversize wood frames, try to process all of·them at once. This way, you can establish a frame stockpile to draw on as you need a frame. Take the frames one at a time, disassemble them, and package them for inventory and future use. By doing this, you'll get a good idea of how many frames you really have—if your original collection is in various stages of disrepair, you may find that there is not as much usable molding as you thought.

TOOLS AND MATERIALS

First, get together all the tools you will need, as illustrated in Figure 4.

Miter Box A wooden miter box, usually of rock maple, is adequate for your purposes, as you will be using the 90° section of it. This kind of miter box is available at hardware stores starting at about $2.

Pliers You will need pliers if there are any nails, tacks, or staples in the old frames. Take these out before using your hacksaw.

Hacksaw You should use the 12-inch blade size, preferably new.

Steel Wool A steel wool pad of the finest texture, known as grade 0000, is desirable for lightly rubbing down

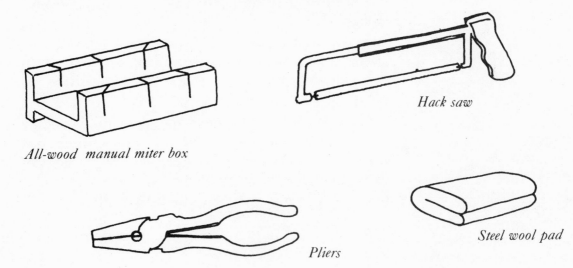

All-wood manual miter box

Hack saw

Pliers

Steel wool pad

Figure 4

the frames to remove any desposits they may have accumulated in years of travel and storage.

Be sure to work on a good, rigid workbench or table. I attach my miter box to my workbench with a vise. Securing your miter box will help you concentrate on the most important things—the molding you are cutting and keeping your hacksaw in an absolutely true vertical position.

THE MITER BOX

There are two types of miter boxes: motorized and manual. The motorized type is more sophisticated than you'll need, unless you're interested in full-time frame making. Manual miter boxes are of either all-wood construction or metal and wood. Wood miter boxes are made of non-warping rock maple (the hardest known commercial wood), but they are not absolutely true, so you need to be very careful when using one in frame making. I use a metal and wood miter box and recommend that you use one too if you intend to make more than a very few frames. Metal miter boxes cost anywhere from about $12 to $100, but they are well worth it. Whether you are cutting 45° cuts in the process of repairing frames or starting out with raw molding to make your own frames, you will find that any mismatch on the corners of your frames has a detrimental effect on your final product.

Use a backsaw with commercially available manual miter boxes. The backsaw is a fine-tooth saw with 11 points to the inch. How much you spend for your miter box will probably determine whether it comes with a backsaw. If you must purchase it separately, the length, whether 16, 24, or 28 inches, will depend upon the size of your miter box. You can use a regular saw with a miter box, but be

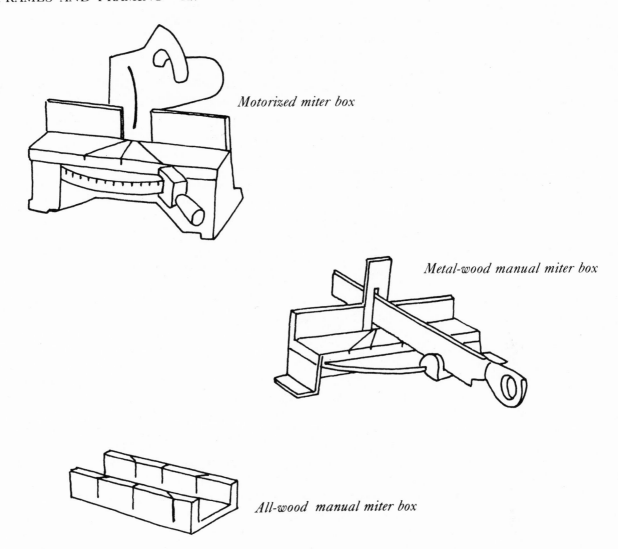

Motorized miter box

Metal-wood manual miter box

All-wood manual miter box

sure it is of the fine-tooth variety, not less than 10 teeth per inch.

If your frame molding is of soft wood, you must use a finetooth saw. With the all-wood miter box, an ordinary 12-inch long hacksaw produces satisfactory 45° miter cuts.

WHAT TO DO: UNMAKING A FRAME

Now we are ready to start. Choose your first frame.

Figure 1

1. Grasp the frame, one hand on each of the long sides, as shown (Figure 1). Now twist. This will partly disjoin each of the corners. By hand, or with a screwdriver, separate the frame into four pieces, two long and two short. Don't concern yourself with the ends of each piece. They will contain nails or will show varying degrees of damage.

2. Take the two long lengths first. Put one in your miter box. Just clearing the 45° miter cut and the nails, cut off one end at 90°. Now do the same with the other end. This your first piece, from which you will measure and cut the second, identical, long piece.

   Cut off the end of the second long piece. Place it alongside the first long piece, and cut off the other end so that you now have two identical molding lengths.

3. Follow the same procedure with the two short

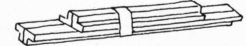

Figure 2

lengths.

4. Tape the four lengths together in a bundle (Figure 2). You now have your first molding package. Proceed with the rest of your frames.

Now, let's take one of these molding packages and work it into a finished frame.

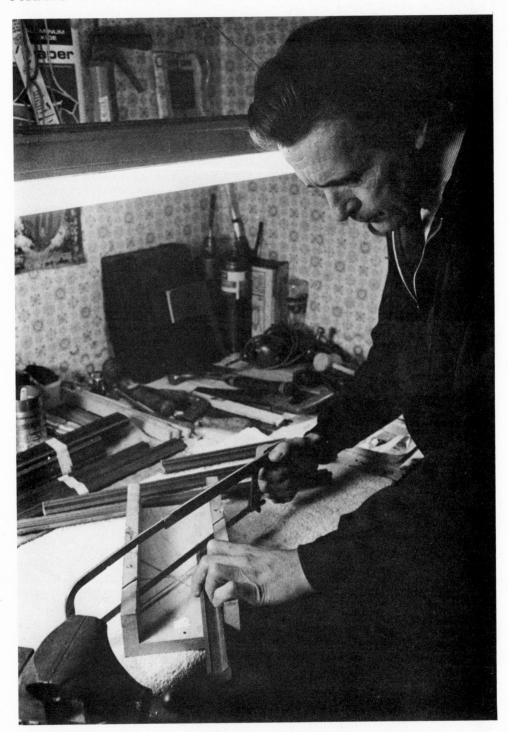

*Frank's frame workshop, with molding package on table (rear) and
Frank working with all-wood manual miter box.*

Table 2

Column 1	Column 2	Column 3	Column 4
Note 1	Note 2	Note 3	Note 4
8 × 10 × ½	6 × 8	5½ × 7½	1
9 × 17 × ¹³/₁₆	7 × 15	6½ × 14½ (Make a 6½ × 8)	1
10 × 12 × ⅝	8 × 10	7½ × 9½	1
12 × 16 × ½	10 × 14	9½ × 13½ (Make an 8 × 10)	1
12 × 20 × ¾	10 × 18	9½ × 17½ (Make an 8 × 10)	1
12¾ × 24 × 1	9¾ × 21	9¼ × 19½ (Make an 8 × 12)	1
14 × 24 × ½	12 × 22	5½ × 10½	2
15 × 18½ × 1½	10½ × 14½	10 × 14 (Make an 8 × 10)	1
15¾ × 24 × 1⅛	12¾ × 21	5⅞ × 10	2
16 × 18 × ¾	14 × 16	13½ × 15½ (Make an 8 × 10)	1
16 × 23 × 1	13 × 20	6 × 9½ (Make a 6 × 8)	2
18 × 23 × ¾	16 × 21	7½ × 10 (Make a 6 × 8)	2
12 frames			*16 frames*

Note 1: This column lists the 12 old frames that I used as a basis for this writing.

Note 2: This column lists the actual length in inches of the 2 smaller moldings and the 2 larger moldings. EXAMPLE: 6 × 8 indicates that we derived 2 pieces 6 inches long and 2 pieces 8 inches long.

Note 3: This column lists the actual finished length of the molding pieces listed in Column 2 *after mitering.*

Note 4: This column lists the number of frames I was able to make, based on the footage I came up with in Column 2.

WHAT TO DO: MAKING A FRAME

Let's start with a relatively complex project—a package from which we'll make two frames. Pick, as an example, the seventh frame down the list. This frame measures

14″ × 24″ × ½″. From this frame came two pieces of molding 12″ long and two pieces 22″ long.

1. Take the first 22″ piece and measure in ¼″ from each end. Place a pencil mark at this point (Figure 1).

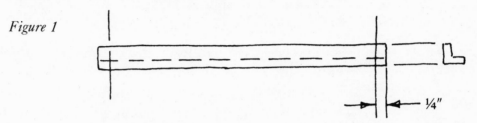

Figure 1

¼″

2. Using your miter box, miter each end 45°, ¼″ in, at your pencil marks (Figure 2).

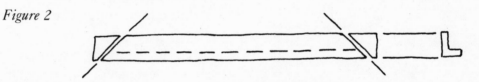

Figure 2

3. After discarding the end pieces, find the exact center line of this molding. Then measure ¼″ to the left of the center line and place a pencil mark there (Figure 3).

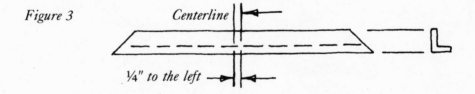

Figure 3   *Centerline*

¼″ to the left

4. At the mark, miter the left-hand piece of molding. You now have the first finished and mitered piece.
5. Matching this piece up with the right-hand piece, place a pencil mark on the right-hand piece. Now miter the other end of the right-hand piece. You

now have two identical pieces of molding. Since the left-hand piece is smaller than the right, it is easy to cut the right-hand piece to match.

6. Follow the same procedure with the other pieces. You now have enough molding to make two frames, both reasonably close to the proportions illustrated in the "Recommended Frame Size Proportion Chart."

As a second example, let's take a frame from which we can only make one smaller frame. Let's use the second frame down the list. This frame measures 9″ × 17″ × 13/16″. From it came two pieces of molding 7″ long and two pieces 15″ long.

1. Take the first 15″ length and measure in ¼″ from each end. Place a pencil mark at these points.
2. Using your miter box, miter each end 45° at the pencil marks.
3. Do the same to the other 15″ length and to each of the 7″ pieces.

You now have four mitered pieces of molding.

Now here is where the "Recommended Frame Size Proportion Chart" comes into use. The molding created from the preceding process would give you a frame 6½″ × 14½″, which is an odd size. The 6½″ pieces suggest that a frame 6½″ × 8″ would be practical. Use the 6½″ pieces of molding as is—don't cut them down to an even 6″.

ASSEMBLY

To assemble these molding lengths into frames, you'll need four basic items (Figure 1).

Frame Assembly Jig Board You can buy corner, miter box clamp sets at your local hardware store, starting at about $12. I made mine for about 35¢. My hardware store

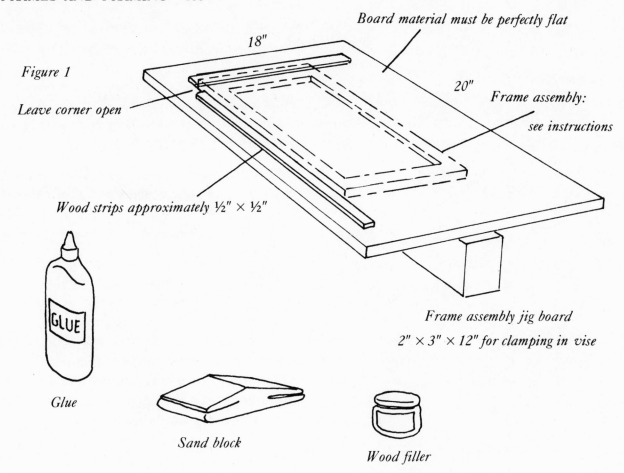

Figure 1

Board material must be perfectly flat

18"

20"

Frame assembly:

see instructions

Leave corner open

Wood strips approximately ½" × ½"

Glue

Frame assembly jig board
2" × 3" × 12" for clamping in vise

Sand block

Wood filler

was selling odd pieces of particle board to which was cemented a thin sheet of formica. I bought a piece approximately 18″ × 20″ for a quarter. The two wood strips I got out of an old window shade. The 12″-long 2 × 3 was an odd scrap piece I had on hand.

To make a similar board, glue the two wood strips to the surface of the board. Use a carpenter's square to make sure they are exactly at 90°.

Leave the corners open. If closed, they will trap glue which will build up and be hard to clean out. To the underside of the board, attach the scrap of wood. This piece of wood will enable you to clamp the jig board into a vise, leaving your hands free.

The formica surface is nice if you can get it because from time to time you can use a single-edge razor blade and scrape off glue deposits that would otherwise keep your frames from being perfectly flat.

Glue I use all-purpose white glue. It usually comes in a handy plastic bottle, and in various sizes—choose the size most convenient for you. White glue dries quickly and is clear and strong. It is available at most stores, from groceries to dime stores.

Sand Block A sandpaper block with a medium-grit sandpaper is a must. Before assembling your four molding pieces on the jig board, check the mitered ends for wood burrs. "Break" the six edges once over lightly (Figure 2).

Note: One of the pitfalls of mitering is that often Surface A (see Figure 2) won't be a true vertical plane. This happens if you don't hold the molding snug enough in the miter box. Correct this before assembling the molding on your jig board.

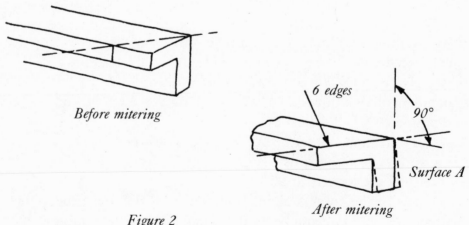

Before mitering

6 edges

90°

Surface A

After mitering

Figure 2

Wood Filler You'll find quite often that after the glue has set on your frame assembly and you remove the assembly from the jig board, some or all of the corners may be imperfect. Hold the frame in one hand and lightly round off the four corners, using your sand block. Apply the wood filler slightly higher than the adjacent surfaces. Let it set for the time recommended on the label, then gently sand with a "round-the-corner" sweep of the sand block.

Final surface finishing of your frame comes next. You will find that in many cases, in order to conceal the filler at the corners, you may have to finger-rub the entire frame with antique gold paste if you cannot match the original color of the finish. In many cases I resorted to painting the entire frame in antique flat black. Finish by buffing lightly.

ON THE JIG BOARD

1. Apply glue sparingly to both ends of each of the 4 pieces of molding.
2. Position one long piece against the wood strip at the left of your board. Follow with one short piece snug against the wood strip at the top of your board.
3. Follow with the final two pieces.
4. Keeping the upper-left corner of your frame snug against the wood strips, press all four corners together tightly.
5. Concentrate on making sure the top surface, or front, of your frame is properly joined and smooth to the touch at each of the miter lines. Let the corners do as they may. They should be reasonably snug or easy to finish off. Remove excess surface glue.
6. Allow frame to set on your jig board overnight.

7. Gently pry up the frame from your board and correct any corner irregularities, as described under "Wood Filler."

Your frame is now ready to be measured for glass. See page 147 for instructions.

SURFACES

Whatever the proportions of your old frames, the surfaces will fall into one of three categories: raw wood, painted wood, and engraved-surface wood frames.

Raw Wood Frames The natural beauty of wood grain is always a joy to the eye. Raw wood frames have an unfinished natural wood surface. Whether it be a coarse-grained hardwood such as oak or chestnut or a close-grained softwood such as pine or spruce, frames of this type are truly worthy of surface restoration if they are otherwise undamaged.

Surface restoration is commonly referred to as "pickling." The aim is to allow the natural beauty of the wood grains to show thru any superimposed finish.

Painted Wood Frames The kinds of soft wood, such as pine or spruce, used in making frames, have a uniformly smooth, grainless wood surface, which is not very interesting. To make up for this their surfaces are usually painted.

Engraved-Surface Wood Frames This type of wood frame is one of the most desirable and valuable of the old frames. The tendency today is toward less ornamentation and less gilt. Just as painters may change their style each year, influenced by fashions, the style of frames also changes, although the change is not as rapid. Today's simpler styles will probably be with us for a while, making the

Color Plate 9   Another picture using only yellow and white flowers. The large flower at the base is golden glow, with daisies, buttercups, grasses, golden rod, butter-and-eggs, larkspur, and raspberry leaves, and elderberry flowers.

Color Plate 10   Oval: spray of grass through middle of picture with the flowers of the shadblow tree, florets of Queen Ann's lace, and sprays of buttercups; A dandelion blossom that turned out well is at the bottom.
Square: focal point is two larkspur flowers, with some field daisies, a viola, and two sprays of leaves with a snapdragon flower on each one. Springing from this are sprays of Queen Anne's lace with larkspur flowers intertwined.

Color Plate 11 Bunny tails growing from a base of leaves and crocus petals; orange cosmos on each side. On top are clarkia and the green stars of the spring bulb star-of-Bethlehem, a good example of thin and medium flowers used together. The daisy-like flowers are from Eleanor Brown's clematis vine. Above crocus petals, a little bunch of the everlasting flower ammobium, not included in my list because it's often too heavy to press.

Color Plate 12 The focal point is a bunch of dusty miller; with candytuft, elderberry flowers, a tomato blossom, phlox, pink and purple larkspur, grasses, pink sage, emilia, and at the very top in the middle, raspberry leaves.

Color Plate 13 The focal point is a buttercup leaf with a chrysanthemum, a spray of goldenrod to the right, and an anemone blanda flower to the right. Springing from this are a blade of asparagus fern, two sprays of mimosa with celandin flowers, a nasturtium and celosia. In the center, a yellow daisy, maidenhair fern, a geranium bud, a hydrangea floret on a Queen Anne's lace circle. To the right and left are blue delphiniums.

Color Plate 14 *Left:* white larkspur, a frond of button fern, Queen Anne's lace, celosia; the little pink sprays are a weed found around here—I don't know its name yet. *Right:* pink and purple larkspur, a cosmos, a spray of Queen Anne's lace, buttercups, and the same pink weed.

Color Plate 15 This frame was given to me fifty years ago by my next door neighbor, Juliana Paca. At that time she told me it was very old, so this is a real antique. I had it wrapped in tissue paper in the attic all these years and never seemed to find the right picture for it. This was one of the most stubborn pictures I ever made. The frame itself is so lovely nothing seemed to fit it. I finally realized that it must have a very simple arrangement because the frame is so ornate. The focal point is a spray of grass, with larkspurs, two sprays of lily-of-the-valley, and some grasses and leaves.

Color Plate 16   The focal point is three cosmos with columbine leaves. To the right and left of the bunch of larkspur are bougainvillea flowers, pressed for me by Glory when she was in Key West. Growing from these on each side is a wild flower found here in the Catskills, bladder campion, with larkspur growing from it.

engraved-surface wood or highly ornamented frame, the gilt frame, a rare and therefore valued possession.

New Frames

New frames purchased through retail stores are made of wood, metal, wood-simulated plastic, or pressed-wood composition, sometimes referred to as "particle" board.

They come with assembly instructions for fastening the cardboard backing into place.

They fit easily into our requirements for pressed flower frames, where we must apply a paper backing to completely seal in our flower composition against dust, moisture, movement, and the effects of atmospheric change.

The plastic frame obtained through such sources is often oval or round in shape. It does pose one problem, however. The rear of the frame, that is, its flange width or thickness, is so narrow and smooth that there is a good chance that the glue you use will not permanently adhere to such a smooth surface and do its job of holding the paper backing in place. It is important, therefore, when using such frames, to take a piece of coarse sandpaper and roughen the entire periphery of the rear of the frame before applying your glue. Remember, white glue is generally intended for bonding porous materials.

Raw Molding Lengths

Local woodworking shops can turn out raw molding lengths to your exact cross-sectional requirements when they are straight cuts (Figure 1) or variations thereof.

Such raw molding lengths involve the routing process,

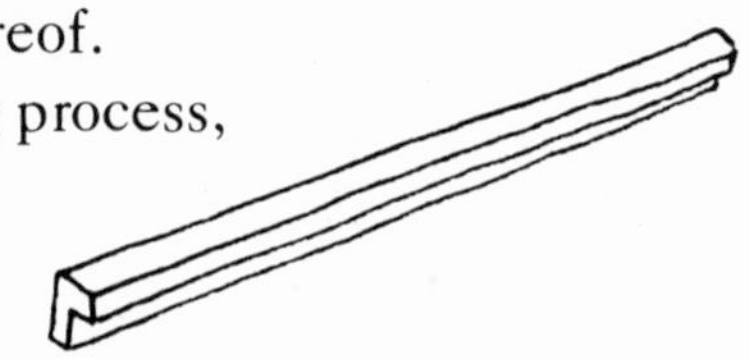

Figure 1   Straight-cut molding

and such woodworking shops have an inventory of routing bits that will produce specific and more artistic cross-sectional configurations, as shown in Figure 3. Refer to

Figure 2   Dimensions of straight-cut molding section

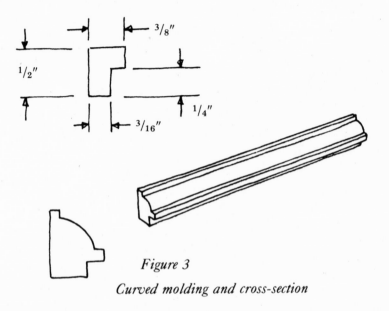

Figure 3

Curved molding and cross-section

mail-order company catalogs to see the routing bits that are available.

Figure 2 is a cross-section view of a frame molding I designed specifically for fabricating 6″ × 8″ frames. I took the sketch to my local woodworking shop and requested 25 molding lengths, each 30 inches long. I specified pine because of it softness. It is easy to work with. The cost was approximately $20. The 30-inch lengths allowed two inches of scrap and gave me leeway in measuring. If you place an order with a woodworking shop, ask for raw or unfinished pine. A number of stains are produced specifically for pine and will give you a variety of light or dark finishes. Charts at your local hardware store will show you how each stain will look on pine; the same stain used on another wood may produce a completely different shade. I have used Minwax No. 230, "Early American," finish and been very pleased with the color. But that is a matter of individual choice, so see what's available.

ASSEMBLY

The assembly procedure is very much like the one you'd use for old frames.

1. Assemble the frame on your assembly jig board (page 132).
2. Apply the stain after removing the completed frame from the jig board, following the manufacturer's directions for applying.
3. After the stain is completely dry, buff it lightly with extra-fine steel wool, grade 0000. Then apply a light coat of fine furniture wax—you can do this lightly with your finger. Let it dry. Buff lightly to a slight gloss. (I use a cabinetmaker's wax produced by the English firm of J. Goddard and Sons in Leicester, England. It comes in several shades—the one I use is called "Sandlewood.")

Glass

I use single-strength glass to protect pressed flower pictures.

CUTTING GLASS

With a little practice and care, cutting glass can be relatively easy. Practice on a discarded piece before cutting

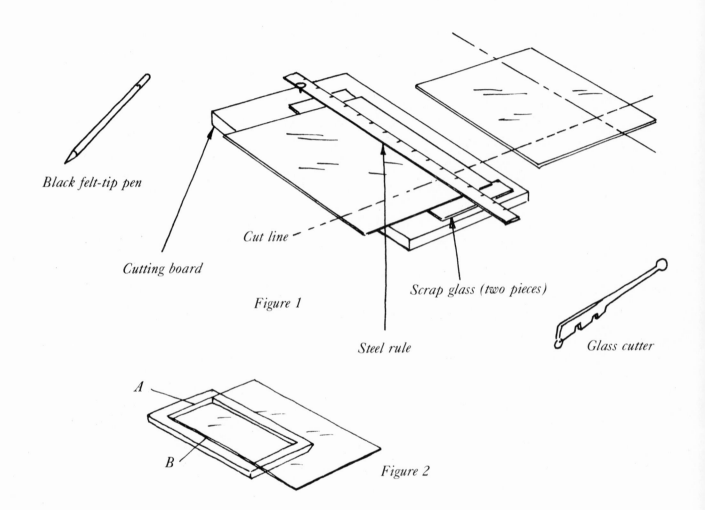

Black felt-tip pen

Cutting board

Cut line

Figure 1

Scrap glass (two pieces)

Steel rule

Glass cutter

A

B

Figure 2

the piece you intended to use. You'll need a black felt-tip pen for marking, a glass cutter, a steel ruler, a cutting board, and scrap glass in addition to the glass you intend to use.

Cutting Board Your cutting board must be smooth and flat. It should be approximately 20 inches by 20 inches and at least ¾ inch thick. I used a piece of particle board to which was cemented a thin sheet of Formica material; I purchased this as an odd-and-end at the local hardware store for 25¢. Install a nail, as shown, at the top center of your board. Your scale will rest against it to ensure your obtaining a perfect cut without any slippage.

Scrap Glass I found it advisable to start my cutter on the top piece of glass and run it off onto the bottom piece of a scrap glass. This ensures a full cut on your good piece of glass. I found also that running the cutter off the end of your glass produced a slight chipping. These bits of glass get into your fingers easily. Use as shown in Figure 1.

1. Lay glass on your inverted frame, carefully positioning it parallel to your frame at A and B, as shown in Figure 2.

2. Now back it off, at A and B, approximately $\frac{1}{32}$ inch. (You don't want it snug.)

3. With your felt pencil, mark the glass at three corners. See Figure 1, which shows glass as marked. Always mark the three corners a little smaller than your frame. It is just about impossible to cut off an excess sliver.

4. Now position your glass on your cutting board as

shown in Figure 1. Make sure the steel rule is resting firm against the nail. Position the scrap glass in position as shown.

5. With all components positioned as shown in Figure 17, press down on the steel ruler firmly with the thumb and forefinger.

6. Starting at the far end and on the scrap glass, draw the glass cutter toward you with a firm, constant pressure, holding the cutter at a slant. Start and stop on the scrap glass.

7. After scoring the glass, place the portion of glass to be removed over the edge of the cutting board (and over the edge of your table). Be sure the score line is close to but past the edge of the cutting board. Apply light pressure and part the glass.

Note: When the portion of glass being removed is narrow, for example, ½ inch, grasp the glass in the center with ordinary pliers and apply downward pressure. Grasping the glass at one end will work also. In other words, when leverage is at a minimum, resort to the use of your pliers.

THINGS TO REMEMBER

· The glass must be perfectly clean. Use any commercially available window cleaning product. This will allow the cutter to glide over it with even pressure.

· Keep the end of your cutter in and lubricated with kerosene before using.

· When you put your glass in the frame, be sure the inside face of the glass is immaculate, free of streaks, smudges, dust, specks, and so on. You have lost access to the inside face once you insert your mounted flower arrangement and secure the backing materials in place.

NOTES ON GLASS SIZES STOCKED IN RETAIL
HARDWARE STORES

My local hardware store gave me the following partial list of sizes, which they try to have in stock. Check with yours to find out what they have. Should you have to buy glass, this partial list will serve as an aid in eliminating unnecessary scrap.

8″ × 10″	12″ × 12″
8″ × 12″	12″ × 16″
10″ × 12″	14″ × 14″
10″ × 14″	14″ × 16″
10″ × 16″	14″ × 18″
12″ × 14″	

Framing

Before you start framing your pressed flower picture, you'll need to have the elements of your flower/frame assembly (Figure 1) and some tools and supplies on hand. Now you're ready to get started.

Figure 1

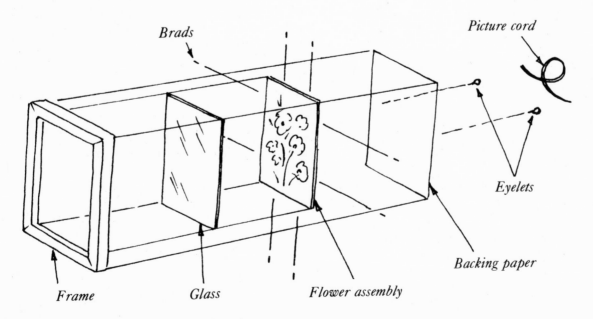

Brads   *Picture cord*

Eyelets

Backing paper

Frame   *Glass*   *Flower assembly*

THE FLOWER/FRAME ASSEMBLY

Cutting Cardboard and Attaching Background Materials

1. Cut the cardboard $1/16''$ less than the frame requires, to allow for the thickness of the background material. (If you're not using velvet, you might make the cardboard slightly bigger—$1/32''$ less than the frame requires, perhaps.)

2. Apply a line of glue as shown (I), approximately ¼" from each edge. With your finger, spread the glue thinly, working it towards the edges as shown (II). Wipe excess glue from your finger with a paper towel.

3. Place the cardboard on the center of the velvet, which is lying face down. (See following section for instructions if you're not using velvet.) The velvet should be ½" larger on each side than the cardboard is. Fold over one side and press down firmly. Pull evenly, firmly on the opposite side, fold over, and press down firmly (III).

4. Lift the four corners of the velvet carefully (IV). Then fold over sides 3 and 4. Pinch each of the four corners, forming a crimp, as shown. Check the front for wrinkles or air bubbles.

5. If the front has passed your inspection, cut off the four corners as shown (V). With a damp sponge go over the velvet lightly, to remove any lint. Press down the four corners firmly.

Background Material Other Than Velvet

In the course of framing pressed flower pictures, we have occasionally come across materials other than velvet that provide a pleasing background. These can be paper, with or without an adhesive backing, and cloth that is lighter in weight than velvet or velveteen.

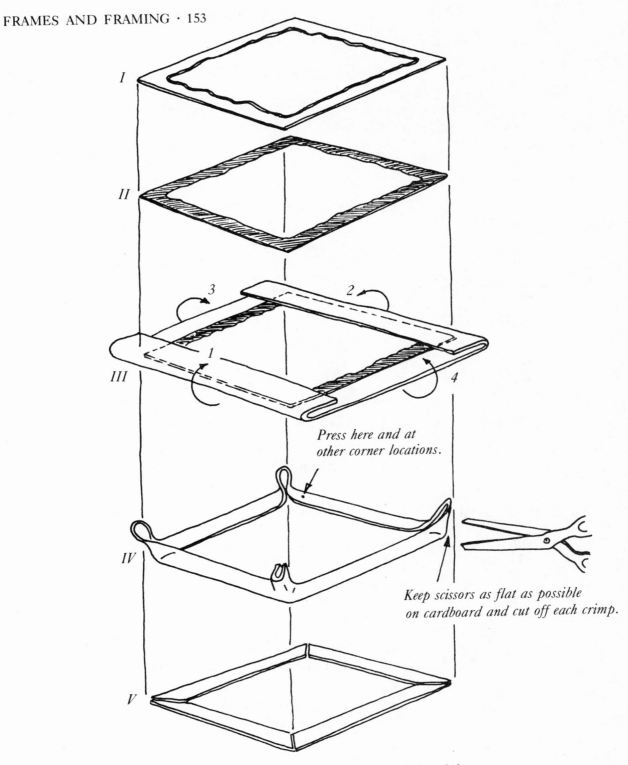

I

II

III

3   2

1

4

Press here and at
other corner locations.

IV

Keep scissors as flat as possible
on cardboard and cut off each crimp.

V

Cutting Cardboard and Attaching Background Materials

One of the materials can best be described as a black, fine-grit sandpaper that is used by the roll in industrial plants for specialized packaging. Unlike sandpaper, however, the surface is velvety to the touch. Once framed and used as a background material, it's hard to tell that it isn't velvet. You might also experiment with a fine-grit black emery cloth or sand paper. Somewhat stiff, it can be successfully attached to your cardboard, provided you get a flat piece without any curl present.

If you use these two papers, here's how to attach them to your cardboard.

1. Apply a line of glue as close to the edge as possible. With your finger, spread it out evenly. Wipe the excess off your finger with a paper towel.
2. Apply your paper background. Leave an excess on all four sides as shown. Pull tight and smooth. Cut off the excess with a sharp razor.

With paper, you do not fold around and onto the back of your cardboard. If you did the paper would tend to balloon out along all four sides of your cardboard, not being as pliable as cloth. Note also that you do not apply any glue to the cardboard anywhere except along the four edges. Even a stray drop of glue would show up on the front surface as an isolated, smooth tight spot if applied, for example, near the center of your cardboard. Another reason for applying glue only along the four edges is that you can pull your paper tight in all directions; it will "give" here and there. Glue applied over the entire surface of the cardboard would have to be spread smooth, a tedious job, and adjustment to eliminate wrinkles would be difficult.

If your paper has an adhesive backing, carefully remove the protective backing and roll on the paper from one end of the cardboard to the other. Smooth out any air pockets. Trim off the excess from all four sides. Do not fold around and on to the back.

If you have found a light-weight cloth other than velvet, apply it to your cardboard the same way you would velvet.

FRAME ELEMENTS: CHECKLIST

Frame This should be in good condition, meeting your standards for construction and finish.

Glass This is the glass that you cut to fit your frame. Check it for blemishes, scratches, chips. Give it a thorough cleaning with spray glass cleaner, and make sure it is completely free of specks, finger marks, and so on. Store it vertically, and preferably under cover until you're ready to insert it into the frame.

Flower Assembly This is the heart of your pressed flower picture—the flowers themselves, securely attached to the cardboard assembly we just described. If you've used a velvet backing (or any other that picks up lint and specks easily), brush it lightly with the corner of a damp sponge to remove the lint.

Brads You'll need eight brads for each picture, two on each of the four sides of the frame. Use ½" No. 18 wire brads, available at your local hardware store.

Backing Paper This is an important element, since it acts as the seal to prevent moisture, dust, and the general effects of atmospheric change from damaging the picture. I use lightweight backing paper, the kind ordinarily used for lightweight packaging. Heavier paper is available, but it is more difficult to work with and less pliable than lighter weight paper. The lighter paper dampens more easily and is less likely to corrugate along each side of the frame.

Eyelets Use ½" eyelets only. Eyelets of this size lend themselves to light frames where the width of the molding is quite limited.

Picture Cord Use only lightweight stranded picture cord. Heavier stranded cord is harder to work with. Unstranded, ordinary lightweight wire will do, but the job will be less professional looking than if you use stranded wire.

TOOLS AND SUPPLIES

Bath Towel At your workbench or table you will need something to cushion your frame as you work with it in the inverted position. A bath towel approximately 24 inches by 36 inches, folded over once, is ideally suited for this purpose. The brads you use will be easier to pick up and be more inclined to stay put when placed on the towel.

Glass Cleaner The spray type of cleaner for glass, kitchen appliances, chrome, Formica, etc., so familiar to all householders, is ideal for your purpose. Available at your local grocery store.

Paper Towels Paper towel rolls are sold under numerous trade names.

Razor Blade Use only single-edge razor blades, available in dispensers holding 10 blades. Use a new, sharp blade at all times. The time and trouble a dull blade gives you is not worth it. You will need this blade to trim your backing paper neatly.

Glue Use a white glue. Usually sold in squeeze bottles, it is inexpensive and convenient to use. White glue grabs well, requiring no mixing.

Pliers Use a conventional pair of pliers. As illustrated, wrap one of the plier "jaws" with masking tape. With pressed flower pictures you do not hammer the brads into the rear of your frame to fasten your flower assembly in place. Rather, you squeeze the brads into their required location with your pliers, placing the protected end, or "jaw," against the outside of the frame, while the other unmasked "jaw" presses the brad gently to the required depth.

Do not secure the flower assembly too tightly against the glass when locating the brads. Make normal contact, otherwise you will notice a "pressure" area in the velvet, which will be evident to the eye in the area of the brads.

Wooden Rule An inexpensive wooden, 12-inch rule with a metal edge on one side is an important tool. Against the metal edge, your single-edge razor will glide smoothly as you trim the backing paper excess off the 4 sides of the rear of your frame.

Cellulose Sponge The convenient hand variety, measuring approximately 4½" × 3" × 1", is ideal. Wet the sponge, squeeze it dry. Available at your local grocery.

Cotton Swabs This type of swab is ideally suited for picking up lint in minute areas on the flower assembly just before assembling the pressed flower picture. Lightly wet both ends of the swab before using. Place it on your towel with the brads and other tools you are using.

Masking Tape Just as cotton swabs are good for picking up lint in minute areas of the flower assembly, masking tape is good for picking up lint in the broader outlying areas. Just cut off one or two inches of your masking tape, hold beneath your forefinger and, using one end at a time, go over any areas showing traces of lint.

This same masking tape is used in preparing the pliers for installing brads.

Scissors Conventional household scissors are all you need. They should be of sufficient size, however, since you will be using them for cutting lightweight cardboard (for the flower assembly) as well as for cutting backing paper roughly to size prior to gluing onto the back of the frame. (I prefer to use a single-edge razor blade or an X-acto knife with a straight-edge.

Ice Pick You will need an ice pick or equivalent tool to pierce the rear of the frame in two locations prior to installing the ½″ eyelets. Whatever tool you use for this should be sharp and have a handle for proper control. Hammering a nail in for this purpose is definitely not a good idea.

Pencil Use a well-sharpened No. 2 lead pencil. You will need it to mark your backing paper and cardboard to size and to locate the position of the eyelets after you have attached the paper.

ASSEMBLING A PRESSED FLOWER PICTURE

1. Place your flower assembly flower side up in the center of the bath towel. For the moment put the frame and glass aside, standing the glass on end to prevent accumulation of lint on either surface. Have your brads and pliers handy.
2. Carefully examine your pressed flower assembly for lint and other extraneous matter it may have picked up. If need be, remove any lint in the more confined spaces with your moistened cotton swab. In the outlying, more open areas, use a short piece of your masking tape. Be sure it passes your inspection in every way. Once the glass is placed over it, it will be inaccessible.
3. Now pick up your glass and examine both sides carefully, under good light, for any last-minute

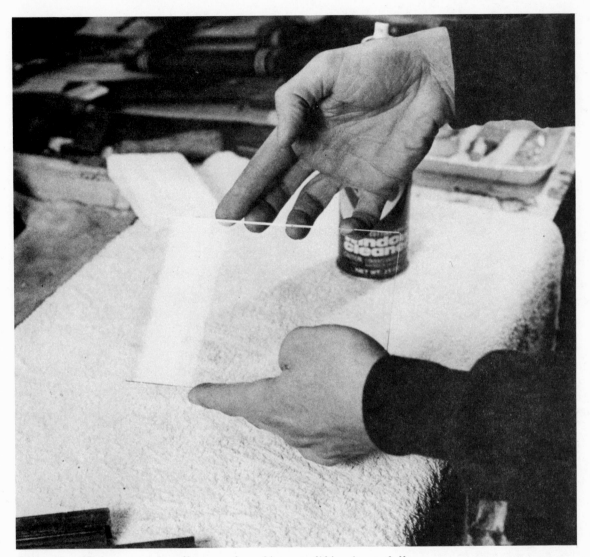

Figure 1   Make sure to handle your glass this way, lifting it carefully at the edges.

lint deposits. Be sure you handle your glass as shown (Figure 1), otherwise there may be new fingerprints or smudges.

4. Carefully place glass on top of your flower assembly. Position it exactly on center (Figure 2).

Figure 2

5. Place your frame directly over the glass and flower assembly combination, being very careful not to move the glass in relation to the flower assembly.

   Since you were very careful in the beginning to cut your glass so that it fitted your frame with ease, your frame should now snap into position. Holding the frame, one hand on each side, gently move it slightly up and down, right and left until you feel it lock into position.

6. With your left and right hands still on each side of the frame, carefully reach under on each side with your fingers and firmly press the flower assembly and glass into the frame. With your thumbs resting on the front of the frame, left and right, you now have the frame package firmly in your grasp. The softness of your towel will enable you to get your fingers underneath the package easily.

7. Carefully invert the entire package and lay it face down on the bath towel. Once in this position, give it a quick check to make sure that the glass and the flower assembly are nestled within the confines of the frame.

8. With your pliers, install your brads two on a side (Figure 3). Gently squeeze the brads into place, making sure the cushioned side of the pliers is against the frame. Before proceeding further, turn your frame right side up and give it a quick check for any irregularity in positioning. The edge of the glass may show if cut too small in the beginning. In such a case, the thickness of the glass edge would reveal an undesirable reflection. Grasping the frame with both hands, gently but firmly move the flower assembly and glass in the required direction. Use your thumbs to move the glass and flower assembly.

Figure 3

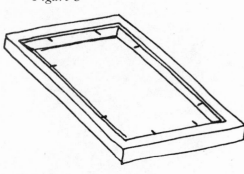

Install your brads two to a side.

Use pliers to squeeze the brads into place, keeping the cushioned side of your pliers against the frame.

Sometimes a piece of lint can appear out of nowhere. Sometimes a speck of one of your flowers can move away and onto the velvet background where it is noticeable. Check for these irregularities before proceeding with the backing paper.

9. Once everything has met with your approval, turn the frame face down on the towel again. You are now ready to attach the backing paper, using your white glue. Apply a line of glue around the four sides of the frame surface to which your backing paper will be attached. In some cases, this surface may be narrow, such as ⅛″; sometimes it may be as wide as ½″ or more. The width will dictate the amount of glue you apply. You want the entire width of the surface to have a thin film of glue after you spread it around with your finger, but not too much, or it will run down the sides of your frame. (See Surface A, Figure 4.)

Figure 4

Surface A

10. Immediately after applying glue around all four sides of your frame, spread the glue around with your finger until you have a thin film the full width of Surface A. Wipe the excess glue from your finger with a paper towel. You are now ready to attach the backing paper to the frame.

11. Cut a piece of backing paper off your roll so that it is 1″ larger than the frame itself, on all four sides. For example, for a frame 8″ × 8″ your paper would be 10″ × 10″.

12. Place the backing paper on your frame, on Surface A, and with your fingers press it down firmly all around. Go around all four sides two or three times. At the same time, grasp the excess material with your left and right hands and pull the paper tight horizontally. Do the same in the vertical direction. Be sure to pull tight and with a downward motion on each side as you pull. This will ensure that your backing paper is adhering smoothly to the edge of the frame when viewed from the side. Otherwise, when viewed from the side, it might appear corrugated or wrinkled.

13. Now you will need your sharp, single-edge razor blade and your 12-inch wooden rule with the metal edge on 1 side. Do not attempt to cut your backing paper off flush with the edge of your frame, otherwise you may find yourself cutting a sliver off the side of your frame, especially if the frame happens to be made of a soft wood. Play it

Place your ruler along the edge of the frame, $^1/_{32}''$ in.

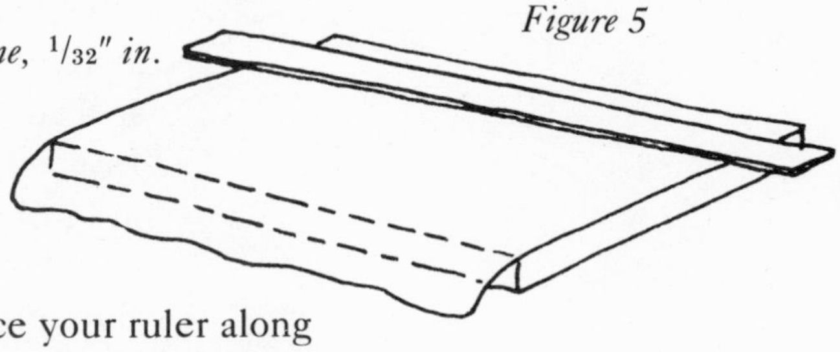

Figure 5

safe. As shown in Figure 5, place your ruler along the edge of your frame, $^1/_{32}''$ in from the edge. With your single-edge razor blade, cut off the excess backing paper. Do the same with the other three sides. The result will be a neat backing job. Also, having come in $^1/_{32}''$, you eliminate the possibility, in handling, of lifting your backing paper away from Surface A of your frame.

14. Looking at your frame from all four sides, look for any corrugating. If it exists, press down firmly, applying a spot of glue if necessary.

15. Now you will need your dampened cellulose sponge. Note that as you examine your frame now, looking at it from all four sides, you will see streaks and areas of glue on your frame sides. Wipe these deposits away before the glue sets. Go back and forth along each side of the frame (Figure 6). Do not be concerned if the edges of your backing paper become slightly moistened. This will serve a purpose—it will be more pliable should you find a last minute "corrugated" condition when you view your frame from the side.

16. Now you will need your ice pick, both ½" eyelets, your picture cord, and your No. 2 lead pencil.

From the top of your frame measure down exactly one-quarter the length of your frame— never more, or it will not hang properly. Mark this point on each side of the frame. With your ice pick, pierce a pilot hole on each side in the exact center of Surface A. Don't make this hole too deep, just enough for the threads of your eyelet to take hold. When Surface A is quite narrow, you must take special care when using your ice pick.

17. Insert your eyelets, one on each side. Screw them in until the eye itself bottoms on the frame. Position each one so that the eyelet is parallel to the side of the frame.

18. Cut a length of picture cord 3" wider than the width of your frame. Attach one end to the first eyelet, giving it two or three full turns. Insert the other end through the second eyelet. Position the "V" of your cord so that it falls at least 1" below the top of the frame (Figure 7).

Fasten the cord to the second eyelet with two or three turns as before. Cut off any excess.

Figure 6

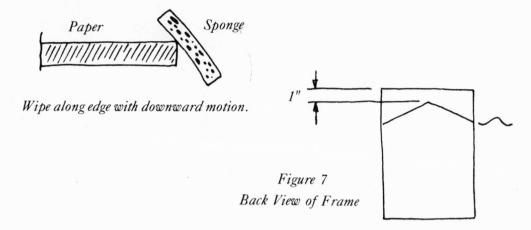

Wipe along edge with downward motion.

Figure 7
Back View of Frame

19. Give your completed pressed flower picture a final examination. If you followed each step carefully, it should be without flaws of any kind. Check your glass for any finger marks or smudges it might have picked up, and wipe it clean if necessary. Now it is ready for hanging.

Mats

If you follow the suggested proportions for rectangular or square frames, you won't need a mat, although you may decide you want to use one. But if you have a frame that is larger than the recommended maximum (see "Recommended Frame Size Chart," page 122), a mat is a good idea.

What size frames lend themselves to the insertion of a mat?

- 8" × 10½"
- 8" × 8"
- larger frames (for example, 12" × 14")

The first two sizes lend themselves to a mat but the effect will be pleasing even if you decide not to use one. For frames smaller than these two sizes, you probably should avoid using a mat, since the combined frame molding width and mat width will be too large in proportion to the picture. For the larger size, you will want a mat to fill out the space.

Mats and mat material are available at art supply stores. Our local art supply store carries two sizes of raw mat material:

Size	Color
20 × 30 inches	White, Tan, Charcoal
32 × 40 inches	White, Tan, Charcoal

They also carry precut mats (about $1/16''$ thick), with the opening already cut out. You need only trim off the outer four sides to fit your frame.

Cutout (Opening)	Color
6 × 8 inches	White, Beige, Gray

CUTTING A MAT

You will need a good cutting tool. It may be a single-edge razor blade, a single-edge razor blade with holder or a craft-hobby knife with a handle (Figure 1).

Single-edge razor blade

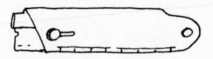

Razor blade with holder

Figure 1

Craft-hobby knife

1. Place the frame face down on the towel you're using. Now measure and cut out your mat. Cut it $1/32''$ short on all four sides so that it drops easily into the frame cavity. This is important—otherwise there is a chance of your mat buckling or not lying perfectly flat. On the other hand, do not cut your mat too small. If you do your mat will shift from one side to the other as well as up and down in the frame.

2. Now that your mat fits easily into the frame cavity with a minimum of movement in any direction, turn it face up, leaving the mat in the frame. With a lead pencil, very lightly draw a line along all four sides of the inside of the frame, as shown (Figure 2).

Figure 2

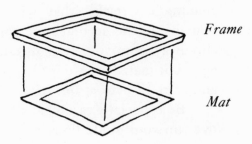

Frame

Mat

3. With the frame lying face up and with the mat still inside the frame, you must, at this point, decide what width of mat you would like around your flower picture. You may want it narrow—1", for example. You may want it wide—2" or 3", for example. There are no specific guidelines as to the width of the mat. The frame size and your judgement as to what looks best should be the determining factors.

4. Now that you have decided on the width of the mat you think will look best, remove the frame from the mat and put it aside.

5. Remove the towel from under the mat and put it aside. During the cutting process you will want a good hard surface under your mat material, a surface that will not "give" as would be the case with the towel underneath.

6. Let us say that you have selected 2″ as your mat width. Measure out 2″ on all four sides from the light pencil lines you made in step 2. This is the area that you will cut out (Figure 3).

7. You are now ready to cut out the center portion of your mat. With a straight edge cutting tool, lightly score around the four sides of the area to be cut out. On this first go-round you are interested only in making a "track" that will guide and contain your blade the second time, preventing a sudden slip away from your straight edge that might damage your mat. If this does happen, discard the mat and start all over again.

Be especially careful at all four corners. Do not overrun your guide lines.

Figure 3

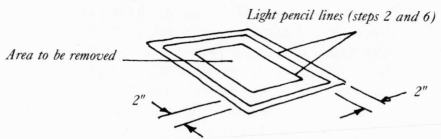

Light pencil lines (steps 2 and 6)

Area to be removed

2″   2″

Go over and over your four guide lines with medium pressure each time as long as it may take before your blade starts breaking through.

You will find that the four corners will be the last to break away. This is because you need to be especially careful in those areas where a slip could mean the end of your mat. I have found that a thin double-edge razor blade carefully inserted at each of the four corners breaks them away nicely.

8. Once the center has been removed, examine each of the four corners for stray bits of mat that you may have to cut away.

The mat is now ready for insertion into your frame, without glass. Insert your background-cardboard assembly behind it. You are now ready to begin arranging your flower composition, centering it carefully within the mat opening.

Different colored mats will have different effects on your pictures. Experiment to see what effects you like best. You might also want to try covering mats with light-weight fabric, to provide added variety or perhaps to complement the colors or lines of a particular flower picture.

TWO FINAL REMINDERS

· In the course of cutting out the center of your mat, you may find that you overran the guide lines at one or more of the four corners. This is very easy to do. Do not discard the mat. Simply draw another set of guide lines ⅛" or ¼" farther out and proceed as outlined in steps 7 and 8.

· There is one disadvantage in using a mat with your pressed flower picture: because of the mat your glass is approximately $^1/_{16}''$ away from the flowers themselves.

This means that when you use a mat you must give added attention to gluing your flowers to the .background. Otherwise when you raise your completed flower picture to the vertical position, as when hanging, the flowers will tend to lean forward towards the glass if they are not properly secured. Any bits of flowers not secured will fall to the bottom.

This is not a problem when no mat is used because the flowers in this case are pressing directly against the glass.

10
The Indispensable Four

Now that you know all about flower pictures and how to make them look their prettiest and last their best, let me tell you about four flowers that I consider just about indispensable, especially if you are just starting. They are Queen Anne's lace, larkspur, pansies, and daisies. With these flowers and some pretty weeds or grasses, you can make lovely flower pictures.

I start Queen Anne's lace, larkspur, pansies, and daisies indoors in March here in New York. When I lived in Maryland I started them in February and sometimes in January, because there they could be planted outside much sooner than here. I plant them early because I cannot wait for spring. At this dreary time of the year I always have a great yearning for green growing things and new flowers for my flower pictures. Planting them early gives me flowers long before I would otherwise have them.

If you have a cold frame so much the better. All of these seeds may be planted in the fall, and this will give you a headstart in the spring. You will have sturdy little plants to put in the garden early, and flowers for pressing long before anyone else.

If you are lucky, sometimes you can get your seedlings to bloom indoors. I have had larkspur blooming in March from an early planting. These flowers seem even more precious when they bloom out of season.

Every year I tell myself that this year I will wait patiently for spring, but I never do. When February comes I begin to feel the urge to plant something. It involves work, because the days are short and there is not much sunshine, so I follow the sun around the house with my boxes of seedlings. They must be carefully watered, fed at intervals, transplanted to individual pots when they get big enough, and gently cultivated. A time-consuming activity, but to me it is worth it. There is also a good side effect. Carrying the boxes and flats of seedlings around gives me lots of exercise and this puts me into condition for spring gardening.

Queen Anne's lace, pansies, and daisies are easy to raise from seed, but larkspur needs some special attention. It is very particular about what it likes and does not like. For one thing, it needs a period of cold to germinate. By cold I mean freezing. If you plant it in a cold frame in the fall this is automatically taken care of. If you plant it inside, you should first put your seed box outside for about two weeks, but cover it to protect it from snow or rain. Or you can put it in your freezer for two weeks and then bring it inside to warmth and light. Larkspur also needs a soil with a little lime in it. I plant it in a soil I mix myself—one part sterilized, bought earth, one part vermiculite or sand, one part peat moss, and some sifted wood ashes. Lime bought at a plant store will also serve the purpose. I use this same mixture for the other flowers but minus the wood ashes. Sometimes I mix in a little dried cow manure.

All of these flowers are tough and can be planted outside in the later part of April. Last year we had a snowstorm after I had planted them outside, and they survived it. I was worried, though, and perhaps I will wait until the first part of May next year. Once planted outside, it does not take them long to start to grow, and you will soon have lovely flowers for pressing.

The ideal method for continued bloom is to plant the seeds directly in the soil as early as it is workable and warmed up. The only flower of these four that may be contrary about this latter planting is larkspur, so to make sure I have enough, I use both methods. With this method, when your first planting has finished blooming, the second planting will be coming into bloom.

Queen Anne's Lace

I suppose you wonder why I cultivate Queen Anne's lace when it grows so profusely everywhere. Here is the reason.

The wild Queen Anne's lace that grows in the fields and by the wayside is a creamy color and the florets are closely packed together. It looks more like lace than the cultivated kind. It also looks somewhat like a little umbrella.

The Queen Anne's lace grown from seed ordered from a seed company has very large, separated florets, which are much whiter than the wild kind. These may be separated and used individually and are very pretty and useful.

There are so many different ways to use Queen Anne's lace. The whole flower can be dried and then cut in half or quarters to make little fans that are more graceful than

the full wheel. (See Color Plate 12.) These fans make wonderful centers of interest, fillers, and lines. They are lovely against dark velvet and provide a perfect foil for brighter flowers.

They can be used in any position—at the top of a picture, at the bottom of a picture, and in the middle. They can even set the mood of a picture. The sparkling white florets create a firecracker effect. They can even seem to be in motion. This flower would be useful for this reason if for no other. Any time you achieve motion in your picture you will really have something. In nature, flowers sway with the breeze, they reach for the sky, and turn their faces to the sun. If you can create this effect, it will be natural and appealing.

The first time Queen Anne's lace blooms, both the cultivated and wild kinds, the flowers are large. Then, as the season goes on, they become smaller and smaller until sometimes you will find some that are quite tiny. This is good, because the large circles can be too large to use by themselves, but the tiny flowers can be used as fillers and to lighten up a picture that may have a tendency to be dark. (See Color Plates 3 and 6.) Queen Anne's lace adds a delicate touch wherever it is used. It falls in graceful lines, and it always looks natural. It is indeed a very obliging flower.

Queen Anne's lace

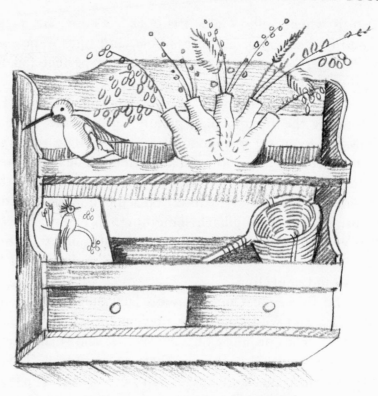

Another combination of a pressed flower picture with Oriental artifacts.

11

Sources of Inspiration

Before you start a flower picture, go to your library. A library is the ideal place to go for inspiration. Books of all kinds can furnish inspiration—books on fresh flower arranging, dried flower arranging, gardening books, books of pictures by famous artists, from which you get a sense of color and design, and wonderful books on Chinese and Japanese art which are supremely inspiring because of the way flowers are included in so many works of art. Study Japanese and Chinese flower arrangements for simplicity and the Flemish and Dutch paintings for mass arrangements.

Books on fresh flower arranging are very helpful. The arrangements are so beautiful, and each one so different, that I am sure you will feel inspired to begin working on your own flower painting. A fresh flower arrangement and a pressed flower painting are completely different fields of endeavor, but they have one important thing in common—flowers. I love to study fresh flower arrangements. The creative ways the flowers are used, and the gorgeous colors make me want to start creating my own flower painting immediately. Not only do they furnish an incentive, but these lovely illustrations teach you the rules of flower arranging in the easiest way—by looking.

My favorite book is *The Art of Arranging Flowers,* by Constance Spry. She was the queen of all flower arrangers. I read an article about her once which I have never forgotten. The author of it said, "when she died a light went out in the world." She is a legend. They say she could take a bunch of weeds and arrange them so beautifully that they would grace the most important table in the world. There has never been anyone like her. So study her arrangements if you possibly can.

What Constance Spry did with fresh flowers you and I can strive to do with pressed flowers. Train yourself to become intensely observant. Look at everything around you with new eyes, and you will feel as though a veil has been lifted. Watch the way things grow in your garden and in the fields. Observe shapes and combinations of colors. Wherever you go make it a game to observe closely all the things you see. It is sad that many people do not see the beauty around them.

Pick one of the flower arranging books that is especially appealing to you—one that you really love. Look at it intensely, study it, keep it where you can see it every day for at least a week. It will become a part of you, and when you begin creating your paintings, even though you may not want to copy it, it will be a part of your consciousness and it will help you to make your own arrangements.

Have you ever read *Elizabeth and Her German Garden,* by Elizabeth? Unless you are my age or are lucky enough to have found the book stuck away someplace in a second-hand book store, you probably have not because not even many libraries have it these days. I love Elizabeth because she dearly loved her garden, and understood the problems of gardening, and shared them with her readers. Her views on gardening seem to me not only to reflect the problems of gardening, but every endeavor on which we may embark.

She says, "Humility, and the most patient perserverance are as necessary in gardening as rain and sunshine, and every failure must be used as a stepping-stone to something better."

Books

ABOUT FLOWERS

Flower Arrangement in Color, by Violet Stevenson. New York: Viking, 1961.

The Art of Arranging Flowers, by Constance Spry. New York: Studio Publications in association with Thomas Y. Crowell.

Wild Flowers of America. Washington, D.C.: Smithsonian Institution. Beautiful illustrations.

ABOUT PAINTING AND ART

A Complete Guidance to Flower and Bird Painting. Hong Kong: Wan Li Book Company.

Chinese Painting, by James Cahill.

Kandinsky, by Jacques Lassaigne. New York: World, 1964.

Kandinsky, by Frank Whitford: Paul Hamlyn, 1967.

The paintings of Kandinsky certainly have nothing in common with pressed flower pictures and yet just looking at them inspires me and makes me want to get to work.

The colors in his compositions fascinate me and makes me want to combine unusual flower colors. The painting "Within the Circle" looks to me like flowers swimming, growing, moving! "Accent in Pink" shows how color forms may be distributed. "Red Spot II" has in the upper-right-hand corner what looks like a glorified Queen Anne's lace and a stylized leaf. And so it goes—each painting has something for me. Pressed flower paintings are compositions in their own way.

Mondrian, by Italo Tomassoni. New York: Crown, 1969.

I frequently take the book of Mondrian's paintings home with me from the library. You may be wondering, "What in the world has Mondrian got to do with pressed flower pictures?" Well, I find two of his paintings extremely inspiring. They are "Flowering Apple Tree" and "Flowering Trees," and the most wonderful study of lines one could ever hope to see. They flow, they move, they are strong and subtle.

Mondrian also painted flowers. I like the watercolor, "Two Marigolds" and a chalk drawing, "Chrysanthemum," and I love the way he uses color—such inspiring combinations.

I am telling you this because I think it shows that you can find inspiration for pressed flower pictures in the most unlikely places.

Van Gogh, by Gerald E. Finley. New York: Tudor, 1966.

Van Gogh's paintings are perhaps the most inspiring of them all. Everyone knows his flaming colors and wonderful designs. My favorites are *Flowers in a Bronze Vase, Oleanders, Sunflowers, Wheatfield with Cypress and Iris.*

Gauguin, by Raymond Cogniat. New York: Abrams, 1963.

Persian Miniatures from Ancient Manuscripts. New York: The New American Library of World Literature, 1962.

Indian Miniatures, by Mario Bussagli. Paul Hamlyn, 1969.

Both of these have gorgeous colors and flower designs used everywhere—on clothing, in the landscapes, as backgrounds.

The How and Why of Chinese Painting, by Diana Kan. New York: Van Nostrand Reinhold, 1974.

Treasures of Asia. New York: World, 1960.

Japanese Stencil Designs, by Andrew W. Tuer. New York: Dover, 1967.

12

Have Fun

I still remember an experience I had as a child as though it had happened yesterday. My brothers and I built a hut in the woods in back of our house. We dragged logs and branches, made little rooms, covered the floor with pine needles. How we worked! I suppose it was a combination of nervous energy and creativity that made the project so fascinating. It was not until I started making flower pictures that I again experienced this feeling of complete absorption and the happiness that comes with creating. This was sixty years later.

For me, pressed flower painting is an absorbing occupation, and the preliminary work of planting, tending to the garden, and picking and pressing the flowers certainly keeps me active and healthy—for which I am grateful.

As I said at the beginning, I never dreamed when I first started making my pressed flower paintings that be-

183

cause of it I would meet many interesting people, make new friends, and do things I had never done before, like display my work at arts and crafts shows. You really must do this—it's fun, and you may even win a first prize, as I did in my second year as a pressed flower artist.

Pressed flower painting is not only a hobby, but a moneymaker if you want it to be. Many kinds of shops—boutiques, gift shops, craft shops, and others—sell pretty, well-done dried flower paintings as unique, one-of-a-kind gifts.

One of the nicest things about this hobby is that it costs practically nothing to get started. This is more than you can say for most hobbies. You can begin with a few pressed flowers, a picture frame you found in the attic or bought at a flea market (most of the ones I have bought cost 25c), a piece of cloth or paper, a nail file, and some tweezers. If you decide to try your hand at color washing you will not need anything more than a child's dime-store box of watercolors, and this also includes a paintbrush—I paid 98c for mine.

Then when you have finished you will need only a small tube of white glue and a piece of brown wrapping paper to finish the back neatly.

On the back you can simply sign it:

An Original
by _____
date

This is what I put on the back of mine:

Flowers picked on a sunny day
In the summer of _____
From the garden of Irene Flesher

So get started and have fun!

Notes

As I work I make notes—for example, "Grow more lilies of the valley next year. I did not realize their little bells could be so attractive. . . . Order a fringe tree in the spring—the flowers look as though they would give good lines." Here are some notes that you may want to remind yourself of as you do your first few flower paintings.

· Save extra pieces of glass left over after framing. They make good palettes for mixing paints. They are also good for putting over flowers that want to curl after color washing. They will flatten them without sticking. Also, save scraps of cardboard for gluing.

· Press some flowers in silhouettes—cosmos can be pressed both ways, open and sideways. Some, like bergamot, press better in silhouette. Be sure and pick lots of buds of roses, larkspur, nasturtium, buttercups with stems and buds, larkspur with sprays and buds at the top.

· Remember that on a picture with a mat you will have to glue more flowers, because a mat holds the flowers away from the glass. Glass plus gluing will hold everything in place, but with a mat the picture is not in contact with the glass, so it will need more support.

Where and How to Display Your Pressed Flower Pictures

There is just one thing you must never do with pressed flower pictures—never hang them where the sun will shine directly on them, because if you do they will surely fade even as draperies and wallpaper fade under the same condition.

A north wall is usually the best location, although there are exceptions. Try them in various places until you find the ideal one. Pressed flower pictures seem to look their best in the kitchen, bathroom, bedrooms, and hallways. Living rooms as a rule have larger pictures, but small flower pictures look very attractive in pairs or groups over a table or desk.

They always look lovely and at home in rooms with flowers as the theme, with fresh flowers or dried flower arrangements; growing plants near them add to their beauty.

I have a pressed flower picture in the kitchen hanging next to a modern painting done by my son Rick. The two pictures have the same yellows and reds, but they are so completely different you would not think they would look good together but they do. They seem to complement each other.

A wedding announcement like this one framed with pressed flowers makes a lovely keepsake.

A friend of mine had two pictures that she could not seem to fit into her living room. She liked them but they seemed too bright or something. She now has one of my flower pictures hanging between them. The pictures look lovely and everyone comments on the arrangement. The flower picture seems to tone down the other two and pull the whole group together.

This is why I think you should keep trying for the best effect—the only way to discover these things is to keep trying.

Pressed flower pictures look especially lovely in bedrooms. I have had people tell me they would like the wall behind their bed filled with them.

Or how about a wall filled with hanging baskets with pressed flower pictures in between?

Or four rather large pictures over a sideboard in the dining room?

A small entrance hall filled with plants and pressed flower pictures?

Lots of little pressed flower pictures in a little girl's room?

You can use pressed flowers to highlight another kind of picture or display. For example, a wedding or birth announcement, done in calligraphy, and framed with pressed flowers, makes a lovely keepsake or wall hanging.

Year-Round Flower Pressing

If you become addicted to pressing flowers as I am you can have a continuous supply twelve months of the year if you plan it right.

The earliest outdoor flowers for pressing are the bulbs, and they can be even earlier if you force them. The ones I like best are the tiny jonquils, snow-drops, lily-of-the-valley, crocus, and the Blanda anemone. You can have these blooming in December, January, and February if you plant them in pots in the fall, leave them outside in a protected place, and then bring them in for forcing as you need them.

If you start some of the annuals inside in March or April you can pick some flowers in May even in this cold climate. You can pick a few before you transplant them into the garden sometimes. I have planted cosmos in the house and picked some for pressing in March. They were even

189

prettier than the outside ones because they were small and dainty and easy to arrange in pictures.

Most of the annuals start blooming profusely in June, so profusely that it is sometimes hard to keep up with them. A garden full of larkspur, daisies, violas, Queen Anne's Lace, pinks, and a few more can keep you very busy. The more you cut them the more they bloom, and you will have a continuous supply the whole summer long into fall.

Many of the wildflowers you grow yourself can be picked quite early, but it seems that the small early ones growing wild are for the most part on the prohibited list. The wild flowers that you are allowed to pick generally do not overflow the fields and waysides until about July, and continue blooming steadily until late fall. Each one has its turn. They last for weeks and give us plenty of time to gather a supply.

Most perennial flowers too have their day. They bloom for their alloted time and then give way to other flowers. Lupines, the evening primrose, and poppies do this. The annual flowers are as a rule more useful for continuous flower pressing.

September is a bountiful month. Every flower seems to be trying to outdo itself before winter catches up with it. And of course this is the month when chrysanthemums begin to bloom; they last until the end of October.

Indoor Plants

When frost comes it is time to move inside. There are many flowering plants that will give you blooms for pressing. True, they will not be as prolific as the outdoor ones, but they seem even lovelier because of this.

Harbingers

Spring too, very soon!
  They are setting the scene for it—
plum tree and moon.

BASHŌ

If you have a sunny window sill many of the flourishing annuals can be dug up, potted, and brought into the house in the fall, and they will continue blooming for a long time. Nasturtiums will live all winter if rooted in water. Chrysanthemums can easily be grown in the house and will flower over a long period. Pinks, daisies, dwarf salvia, most herbs, and ageratum are some of the ones you can bring inside. I am sure anything can be made to grow and bloom in the house if given the proper care.

I always have a few flowers on my houseplants that I can pick and press in the winter. Geraniums, African violets, columnea, begonias, and kalanchoe bloom all winter. Not only flowers but the foliage of many house plants press very well—palms, ferns, geraniums, grape-leaf ivy (in fact all the ivies), baby's tears, creeping fig, and coleus are just some.

Another way to get flowers early is to force some bare branches from your shrubs in water. This is easy to do—in a short time after being brought into the warmth of the

Mountain Plum Blossoms

With the scent of plums
on the mountain road—suddenly,
sunrise comes!

BASHŌ

house they will burst into bloom, and you can pick some of the blossoms for pressing. Forsythia, all fruit trees (apple, plum, cherry are excellent), spirea, and flowering quince are among the branches you can force.

Indoor plants and flowering branches and pots of bulbs in bloom serve a double purpose. They brighten winter rooms as well as giving us material for pressing. I would not want to be without them. They help me to bear the long, cold winter months, they keep the air moist and fresh and fragrant, and they keep me company and give me hope that spring will come again.